COPING WITH POPULATION
CHALLENGES

COPING WITH POPULATION CHALLENGES

Louise Lassonde

In collaboration with the
Laboratoire de démographie
of Geneva University

Translated from the French
by Graham Grayston

Earthscan Publications Ltd, London

First published in the UK in 1997 by
Earthscan Publications Limited

First published in France in 1996 by
Éditions La Découverte, Paris

A catalogue record for this book is available from the British Library

ISBN: 1 85383 420 3 paperback
ISBN: 1 85383 435 1 hardback

Typesetting and page design by PCS Mapping & DTP, Newcastle upon Tyne

Printed in England by Clays Ltd, St Ives plc

Cover design by Andrew Corbett

For a full list of publications please contact:

Earthscan Publications Limited
120 Pentonville Road
London N1 9JN
Tel: (0171) 278 0433
Fax: (0171) 278 1142
Email: earthinfo@earthscan.co.uk
WWW: http://www.earthscan.co.uk

Earthscan is an editorially independent subsidiary of Kogan Page Limited and publishes in
association with WWF-UK and the International Institute for Environment and
Development.

For
Barbara Vesely
Catherine Garcia
Tara M'Hamdi
Vera Sipova

Contents

Tables and Figures

Tables

Figures

Abbreviations

AID	Agency for International Development
DDC	Direction du développement et de la coopération
FAO	Food and Agriculture Organization
GNP	Gross National Product
INED	Institut national d'études démographiques
IUSSP	International Union for the Scientific Study of Population
OECD	Organisation for Economic Co-operation and Development
PAPD	Programme of Action on Population and Development
UN	United Nations
UNCED	United Nations Conference on Environment and Development
UNCTAD	United Nations Conference on Trade and Development
UNFPA	United Nations Population Fund
WHO	World Health Organization

Acknowledgments

This book was written on the initiative of the Direction du développement et de la coopération (DDC) of the Swiss Federal Department of Foreign Affairs, and with its support. It was planned in collaboration with Geneva University's Laboratoire de démographie économique et sociale, which studies population dynamics to identify their implications for societies and individual behaviour. It is a contribution to the dissemination of knowledge about population trends and to discussion of their challenges, and is part of the Laboratoire's work with the DDC. Assistance has been provided by the International Union for the Scientific Study of Population.

I should like to thank those individuals who have helped with this book from its inception: Olivier Chave (DDC), Claudine Sauvain-Dugerdil and Hermann-Michel Hagmann (Laboratoire de démographie économique et sociale, Geneva University) and Jean-Claude Chasteland (Institut national d'études démographiques (INED)).

I am also grateful to those people whose informal exchanges of ideas with me or specific comments have enriched this work: Sarah Adams, Alaka Basu, Giuseppe Benagiano, Pierrette Birraux-Ziegler, John C. Caldwell, Pat Caldwell, Martha M. Campbell, Jose Albert de Carvalho, Josette Coenen-Huther, Philippe Collomb, Pierre Cornillon, Jane Cottingham, Nicolas Felder, Jerome Grossman, Werner Haug, Allan G. Hill, Claudine Hodgens, Johan Holmberg, France Jans, Hans de Jonge, Jean Kellerhals, Jacques Légaré, Peter Van Look, Michel Loriaux, Miroslava Macura, Carla Obermeyer Makhlouf, Alain Marcoux, Jacques Martin, Walter Mertens, Axel Mundigo, Simon Newman, Christine Oppong, Elena Permato, James Phillips, Christine Pintat, Jean-Yves Pouilloux, Harriet Presser, David Reher, Bruno Remiche (†), Gilbert Ritschard, Paul Sauvain, Peter Sich, Mathias Stiefel, Dominique Tabutin, Georges Tapinos, Jacques Vallin, Jane Verral, Carl Wahren, René Wéry, Basia Zaba.

Thanks are also due to Beata Godenzi, who helped me with document research; Yves Rémond, who provided the illustrations; Prayat Punong-ong, the *Far Eastern Economic Review*, the *South China Morning Post* and *The Straits Times* for permission to reproduce excerpts; and *Courrier international*, which gave permission to reproduce excerpts from the international press.

This book is the fruit of discussions with experts in various fields. Their contributions encourage readers to consider various aspects of the population issue which require closer analysis. I extend to them all my special thanks for their interest in this collective project:

Joaquín Arango, sociologist; director, Centro de Investigaciones Sociológicas, Madrid

Joel Jakubec, pastor, Église nationale protestante de Genève

Ronald Jaubert, economist; teacher/researcher, Institut d'études du développement, Geneva

Thérèse Locoh, demographer; director of research, INED and Centre français d'études sur la population et le développement, Paris

Alfred Perrenoud, demographer; professor, Département d'histoire économique, University of Geneva

Gonzague Pillet, economist, professor at the Universities of Fribourg and Alexandria

Jean-Paul Porterie, economist and demographer, consultant to international organizations on population, environment and development issues

Claudine Sauvain-Dugerdil, anthropologist and demographer; maître d'enseignement et de recherches, Laboratoire de démographie économique et sociale, University of Geneva

Walter Stahel, architect; director, Institut de la durée, Geneva

Jacques Vicari, architect and archaeologist; director, Centre universitaire d'écologie humaine, Geneva

Anne Zwahlen, teacher and ethnologist; officer-in-charge, Programme développement équilibré homme–femme, DDC, Bern.

Introduction: A New Perspective

Population concerns reappear without any prompting at a time of political turmoil, economic instability or identity crisis. At the international level, the population issue was given a new lease of life in the 1970s when a population explosion was said to be imminent – what was called the *P bomb*, another of the spectres haunting the Western world. Initially, population growth was alleged to cause underdevelopment; later, as people became aware of environmental degradation, it was said that it could ruin our planet. Now, however, the population growth rate is declining worldwide. Yet despite this decline and a considerable reduction in fertility, except in a few countries (particularly African ones), the problems are far from being resolved. In fact, the momentum of past growth will have almost doubled the world's population by the middle of the next century. We shall therefore have to find ways of coping with a very difficult fifty-year period.

In the light of what is looming on the horizon of the third millennium, it is increasingly clear that the new demographic challenges cannot be understood and addressed in Malthusian terms, with the focus on a balance between the number of human beings and available resources. A new approach is needed, one which is normative and qualitative, i.e. ethical. Just as the scale of the problem has changed, so has its nature. The heart of the population problem now lies in our commitment and our ability to build a sustainable world for ten billion human beings.

The challenges ahead are the relationships between individuals, generations and peoples, and between the human race and nature. The ethical and pragmatic requirements involved are respect for differences and maintaining the diversity of individuals, cultures and forms of life. This entails redefining political relationships and the economic system, starting from the premise that the welfare of mankind is of supreme importance.

There are indications that we have reached a watershed in our approach to the population issue. As certainties collapse at the end of an era, signs heralding a new one are sought. Its beginnings are often vague and difficult to interpret. At first sight, it is the international political debate – not science and scientific method – that seems to be ushering in a new period. There are parallels between the 'sustainable development' debate and the international population debate. With hindsight, it is clear that the United Nations Conference on Environment and Development (UNCED, more commonly known as the Earth Summit) marked the climax of environmentalism in the narrow sense of nature conservation. It is also clear that it was the starting point for much positive thinking and an abundance of initiatives to transform the economic production process, amend legislation and establish new, partnership-based relationships between representatives of governments, the private sector, universities and local communities. The sustainable development debate has brought about these changes by requiring the economic system to 'address the full complexity of the world and that of mankind in all its psychological, social and biological dimensions, not the caricature known as *Homo oeconomicus*'.[1]

With regard to the international population debate, the International Conference on Population and Development, held in Cairo in 1994, may be regarded as a turning point. Although the public debate was monopolized by supporters and opponents of abortion, the international community adopted a wide-ranging programme of action containing many new elements as well as a number of unresolved issues. It is these issues that require a review of demography's purpose and analytical tools in order to throw more light on the challenges of the next fifty years.

The Cairo Conference also had a significance which transcended its subject matter, deriving from the context of international relations in the last decade of this century. There have been intensive negotiations in the 1990s: the Children's Summit in New York, 1990; the Earth Summit in Rio de Janeiro, 1992; the Conference on Human Rights in Vienna, 1993; the Conference on Population and Development in Cairo, 1994; the Social Summit in Copenhagen, 1994; the Women's Conference in Beijing, 1995; the Habitat Conference in Istanbul, 1996; and the World Food Summit in Rome, 1996. A growing number of delegates have attended each conference, invitations having been extended to new categories of participants with little or no involvement in international negotiations. These include members of parliament, non-governmental and community organizations, business leaders, local communities and the media. As well as doing their usual work, the media in some cases transformed the conferences by giving the debates an impact which the organizers had neither hoped for nor expected.

There was a growing realization at all these gatherings that the way of conducting negotiations had reached a turning point and that this series of major conferences was the swansong of the 'conference system inherited from the nineteenth century'.[2] Since the creation of the League of Nations, international organizations have globalized politics. Now that nearly every sphere has been globalized and there are recommendations on nearly every subject, we must 'discover not the way to create new conventions, but the way to secure compliance with those that already exist'.[3]

Twenty years after adopting the first World Population Plan of Action in Bucharest in 1974, the international community adopted in Cairo a 20-year Programme of Action on Population and Development. It is an important milestone insofar as the actors concerned may point to states' commitment to implementing its recommendations. This book examines the Programme in the light of the challenges of past and present demographic change for states and individuals, and their implications for action.

Chapter 1 outlines the history of the population debate; the ideological conflicts and alliances during the drafting of the Programme; and the political context of the negotiations. Chapters 2, 3 and 4 discuss the Programme's main topics. First, its principal recommendations are summarized in language as close as possible to that of the official document. The advantages of this are twofold: newcomers are initiated into the sterile and unavoidably repetitive United Nations jargon, and those working in the population field are provided with a source of reference. Next, the progress made is described – new subjects which have been introduced into the debate, and new approaches to subjects discussed at previous conferences. Lastly, a number of important but neglected aspects are highlighted which are not dealt with in the Programme of Action, or if so, only superficially. They reveal what remains to be formulated or achieved in the international population debate.

Chapter 5 examines the measures and machinery for giving effect to states' commitments. Chapter 6 assesses the negotiations, emphasizing the differences in perspective and interpretation as regards their results. It also draws attention to some of the inconsistencies that will need to be resolved if the Programme is to be implemented. Chapter 7 identifies the Programme's implications and puts forward some ideas for reformulating problems and defining the appropriate economic framework for solutions. The concluding chapter brings to light the underlying ethical dimension of all choices relating to the population issue.

Chapter 1
Points of Reference

The History of the Population Debate

The population debate is not a new one. It appeared in its modern form as long ago as the eighteenth century, the specific issue being the relationship between population and means of subsistence.[1] Starting out as an intellectual matter, population eventually became the subject of international political prescriptions. Developments were spread over three main historical periods.

1853–1944: A New Subject

The first scientific population conference was held in Brussels in 1853, on the initiative of Adolphe Quetelet, to perfect census-taking methods. It was followed between 1876 and 1912 by numerous meetings dealing with the relationship between population and hygiene. In 1927, Margaret Sanger, a pioneer of family planning, organized on her own initiative a conference in Geneva which led to the creation of the International Union for the Scientific Study of Population (IUSSP), the main body for professionals interested in the links between demographic phenomena and social development. During the inter-war period the experience and problems of the European continent were the sole focus of interest in the population debate. This debate took place with war on the horizon and against a background of fears about a decline in population. Until the 1950s there were two major areas of concern: migration due to localized overpopulation, and family planning, which was viewed as an individual right potentially at odds with the common interest.

1945–1965: An International Dimension

The end of the Second World War marked a turning point in the scientific and political approaches to population, and in particular saw the US emerge as the main player in both areas. According to Jean-Claude Chasteland, of the three principal population actors that appeared on the scene in the US during that period (foundations, government and scientists), the foundations[2] were the pioneers. This is because they were the first to consider the political and social implications of world population growth.

The other key element in this period was the establishment of the United Nations, which gave the debate an international setting. Among the specialized UN bodies created was the Population Commission, set up in 1946 to deal with population issues multilaterally. It now has a membership of over 170 states, and its secretariat is provided by the UN's Population Division, whose main function is to prepare world population projections and carry out studies of population dynamics trends and impacts. Following the Cairo Conference, it was recently renamed the Population and Development Commission to reflect the widening of its sphere of competence.

This second stage, of great political importance, also witnessed many scientific developments: the refinement of demography's main methodological tools; the completion of an initial study of population dynamics factors and impacts which established a link between population and socioeconomic parameters; the development of empirical research; the structured training for demographers; and the finalization of the UN Population Division's first worldwide population projections. In 1954, the UN and the IUSSP held a conference in Rome under the auspices of the Food and Agriculture Organization (FAO) to promote the collection of statistics, most particularly in developing nations. At a completely different level, the conference's purpose was to hold a rigorous scientific debate to correct what G. George-Picot termed in his opening address 'erroneous beliefs' and to sensitize decision makers to population issues. A similar conference was held in Belgrade in 1964. It drew the international community's attention for the first time to fertility's role as a socioeconomic factor in development. More than 450 experts participated in the Rome conference, and more than 900 in the Belgrade one.

By the end of this period the main challenge posed by demographic change had become clear. Refinement of analytical methods and the multiplicity of subsequent ideological stances would enrich the debate, but the crux of the matter would remain the same: 'The importance of population growth over the next 25 years transcends economic and social considerations. It is at the very core of our existence'.[3] These sombre words reveal that as long ago as 1959 some people were already aware of the need to view demographic change in close conjunction with changing lifestyles, the various social options and the dynamics of relations among peoples.

1966–1994: Population at the Centre of the Political Debate

The United Nations General Assembly resolution 2211 of 1966 called for training centres to be established, and for pilot schemes to guide the developing countries in devising and implementing 'population' programmes. To carry out that task, in 1967 the UN set up a trust fund that began operating in 1969 under the name of the United Nations Fund for Population Activities (UNFPA).[4] In 1972, after a considerable increase in funding and the number of programmes, the Fund was placed under the direct authority of the General Assembly.[5]

Between 1974 and 1994 the UN held three population conferences: in Bucharest in 1974, in Mexico City in 1984 and in Cairo in 1994. These marked a break with the past – they were political, not technical – and their purpose was not to take stock of the situation or of the lessons to be learnt from it. With each conference the scientific debate became less important, a development paralleled in other UN fora. States' representatives discussed political trends and adopted measures designed to be implemented by each nation. The Bucharest Conference ended with the adoption of a World Population Plan of Action, which was reviewed ten years later in Mexico City without any significant changes to its structure or main thrust. The Cairo Conference adopted a Programme of Action extending over 20 years (1995–2015), which replaced the 1974 Plan.

The Ideological Context

The three population conferences were held in very different ideological contexts. The Bucharest Conference was held at the industrialized nations' request. In the light of the proposed New World Economic Order, the issue was whether fertility reduction would promote economic development, or vice versa. The countries of the South – the G77 group – stressed the primacy of development, whereas the industrialized nations argued that without family planning and fertility reduction the South's economies would be unable to take off.

3

The Mexico City Conference was held at the request of the developing countries. They were beginning to feel most acutely the effects of their high population growth, and therefore wished to draw the international community's attention to their financial and technical assistance needs. It seemed that the Conference would be consensus-based, but suddenly the US adopted a position radically different from its approach in 1974. It argued that population growth was a 'neutral phenomenon' in itself, and that underdevelopment's causes lay in excessive economic centralization, which placed artificial constraints on the market. The American argument, which was directed wholly against the communist and socialist systems, was based on the idea that population growth can be accommodated insofar as the markets function properly. The goal to be pursued – economic development – must remain the same, but population growth reduction was no longer a prerequisite. Instead of fertility reduction, the US advocated free trade, the entrepreneurial spirit, international aid and diversification of investment sources. In Cairo, however, the approach was completely different, the issues being those of the 1990s: in particular, gender inequities, action to combat poverty and, at the opposite end of the spectrum, religious- and identity-based movements.

Fault Lines

Each conference produced a different ideological fault line: North–South in Bucharest and East–West in Mexico City. In Cairo, proponents of a secular concept of society clashed with proponents of a theocratic concept. In the opinion of Joaquín Arango, the main dispute in Cairo was between the supporters of individual reproductive and sexual rights, and those who believe that states are entitled to restrict such rights in the name of cultural values and religious beliefs.[6] The acrimony between the two sides was partly due to the subject itself: life, death and sexuality are highly emotive issues and discussing them in an international forum is a daunting task. What exacerbated matters, however, was the sheer strength of the women's movement, which had not previously been in such a good position in international negotiations.

Mobilized as never before in the population debate, the international women's movement made good use of that position to form a remarkably effective alliance with other interest groups. The Cairo Conference's organizational structure provided it with the three prerequisites for success: the support of the 'population group', the main pressure group and the most experienced population conference participant; the support of the US Government, the most important player in the negotiations; and the support of the Conference's Secretary-General, who was willing to bring all her influence to bear on the preparation of the Conference in order to highlight women's problems.

Alliances between Interest Groups

The 'population group' is an internationally oriented movement of American origin comprising representatives of universities, government, non-governmental organizations and the media. Its relations with the women's movement reached a turning point at the Earth Summit in Rio. Contrary to a commonly held belief, that gathering discussed the population aspect of sustainable development and even devoted a separate chapter to it in its Programme of Action, known as Agenda 21. Feminists and population group members clashed over the relevance of 'population' at an environment conference. The feminists alleged that the population group was preventing improvement of women's status, because promotion of family planning amounted to accusing women – even the wombs of women (sic) – of being responsible for destroying the environment.

To reduce the influence wielded by the population group, the women's movement agreed on a common approach with the Vatican to restrict the scope of the sole family planning recommendation in the Programme of Action. This tactical agreement was a success, particularly since the government usually quickest to advocate family planning – the US Government – did not wish to enter the fray. For domestic political reasons, the Bush administration had no desire to champion the feminist cause in the international arena. Moreover, since the population recommendations had been presented by the Conference secretariat as the political counterpart of the recommendations on production and consumption patterns, the US was unwilling to go any further than it had already gone, so as to avoid being forced to compromise in the economic sphere. After all, had not George Bush gone to Rio to proclaim loud and clear: 'The American way of life is not negotiable'?

The Rio Turning Point

After the Rio Conference relations between the two groups changed radically. To prepare for the population conference, the women's movement started an intense dialogue with the population group. Both sides sought to find common ground and a common language to reconcile their concerns, so as to make themselves more of a force to be reckoned with in the intergovernmental negotiations. In an in-depth analysis of the ideological stances and means of action of the groups involved in the population debate, Martha Campbell[7] has shown how an alliance was achieved. It required the population group to cease giving priority to family planning and instead to support the priorities of the women's movement – women's health, rights and status. The two groups then adopted a common approach and language expressed in the 'reproductive health' concept (see Table 1.1).

5

Table 1.1 *Interest Groups' Priorities*

Population Group	Women's Group
1. Ample and well-designed family planning programmes.	1. Ending women's persistent poverty and dependence.
2. Opportunities for women: education, income, health, credit, property rights.	2. Obtaining for women access to education, opportunities, credit, property rights and good health care services.
3. Reduce poverty through improved distribution of wealth and opportunity.	

Source: Campbell, 1993[8]

This alliance between two different interest groups, created and – generally – led by American feminists, who exercised 'discreet tutelage'[9] of the feminist movements from the countries of the South, largely ousted the other players from the centre of the debate. The demands of the women's movement suddenly entered the population debate just as the Clinton administration was staking part of its domestic political capital on support for the feminist cause. In so doing, it was clearly departing from the muted position of the Bush administration's representatives at the Rio Conference two years earlier. A *de facto* alliance was thus formed between the main political player in the negotiations – the US – and the non-governmental organizations in the population group and women's group. As a result, the non-governmental women's organizations were able to play a major part in drawing up the Programme of Action and to influence the negotiations directly since they had 'secured a significant number of places'[10] in the main government delegations.

The Structure of the International Negotiations

The Pains and Pleasures of Consensus at Any Price

In the symbolism of international conferences, consensus does not mean unanimity. The idea of consensus is essentially an indicator of the spirit prevailing in negotiations and the desire of states to arrive at a declaration of common intent despite potential disagreements on specific matters, about which they may enter their 'reservations' (Table 1.2). In that connection, the French daily newspaper *Libération* noted that by endorsing only part of the Programme of Action, the Vatican had invented a new diplomatic concept – 'partial and incomplete consensus'.[11] Consequently, although the Programme of Action on Population is a consensus document, 20 states entered various reservations on religious grounds. Those states are as follows: Argentina, the Dominican Republic, Ecuador, El Salvador, Guatemala, the Holy See, Honduras, Malta, Nicaragua, Paraguay and Peru (Catholic states); and Afghanistan, Brunei Darussalam, Egypt, Iran, Jordan, Libya, Syria, the United Arab Emirates and Yemen (Islamic states).

The adoption of a programme of action is essentially a moral undertaking by states. This is because, unlike a convention, which commits them in law, it is non-binding. To secure the endorsement of such a programme by nearly 180 states, negotiating techniques have to be used which enable a reasonable degree of agreement to be reached, but at the same time leave enough room for interpretation so that each government believes that it has derived some benefit. Three techniques are central to any agreement; they appear to have been used systematically in the international negotiations of the 1990s. We shall term them the principles of juxtaposition, imprecision and specificity.

The Principle of Juxtaposition

To move negotiations forward and sort out any conflicts over a particular recommendation, participants juxtapose positions rather than eliminating the contradictions entailed by opposite proposals. In the Cairo Programme, various formulations which were contradictory *a priori* were worded in such a way as to satisfy all parties. This is what happened in the controversy over abortion, which was circumvented by means of a wording that satisfied all groups. It reads as follows: 'In those circumstances where abortion is not against the law, such abortion should be safe'. In other words, safety (and therefore the possibility of an abortion) is not relevant where a government regards abortion as unthinkable. Safety is recommended, however, where abortion is not unthinkable. Consequently, since all positions on abortion are given equal weight, the wording agreed upon satisfies both those who wish abortions to be safe and those who do not want to acknowledge their legitimacy except in specific circumstances spelt out in their domestic legislation. Although these wordings are sometimes convoluted and disconcerting for those not participating in the negotiations, they are of vital importance. This is because they express a concept which is particularly effective since it is deliberately charged with a multiplicity of meanings, and so makes it possible to break a deadlock in negotiations.

Table 1.2 *Reservations*

Subject	Reasons
Terminology	
Person; individual	The recommendations must refer to the man/woman as a married couple; too individualistic conception of sexuality; not in conformity with Islamic Sharia; risks of misunderstanding; not in conformity with the American Convention on Human Rights and relevant civil and criminal law.
Couple	The concept is unacceptable if it refers to two persons of the same sex or if it covers individual reproductive rights outside marriage and the family; risks of misunderstanding.
Family	Only a family based on the union of a man and a woman, and a single-parent family, can be recognized; the parents' right to rear their children and protect the family must be affirmed.
Reproductive health	New, ambiguous term requiring further analysis; cannot encompass abortion as a fertility regulation service or method; voluntary termination of pregnancy is illegal; certain family planning methods are morally unacceptable; risk of being in contradiction with domestic law, respect for human beings, Islamic law, moral values and cultural traditions.
Abortion	Definition lacks clarity; maintains the illusion that an abortion can be performed without medical, psychological or other risks; not in conformity with religious beliefs; illegal act; denial of the unborn child's rights.
Principles	
Right to life	Recognized from the moment of conception according to the American Convention on Human Rights; is the basis of all rights; in contradiction with Islamic Sharia.
Reproductive rights	In contradiction with Islamic Sharia, domestic law, and moral and cultural values.
Equity in inheritance	Not in conformity with Islamic Sharia and contrary to the principles of Islamic law.
Measures	
Sex education and family planning services for adolescents	In contradiction with some countries' fundamental principles; educational content must be defined by parents to prevent moral perversion and mental illness; in contradiction with Islamic Sharia, moral values and cultural traditions.
Supply of contraceptives to prevent sexually transmitted diseases	In contradiction with Islamic Sharia, and with some countries' moral values, cultural traditions, domestic law and fundamental principles.
Abortion	Only abortion on grounds of medical necessity is justified.

The Principle of Imprecision

Some subjects require imprecision more than juxtaposition. This is particularly true of the new ideas that serve as a framework for debate – for example, the idea of sustainable development. By setting as their objective 'sustained economic growth in the context of sustainable development' states avoid the awkward inconsistencies between the concepts of economic growth, sustainable social structure and environmental carrying capacity. The wording suits both those who maintain that only growth will solve unemployment problems and meet a growing population's basic needs, and those who argue that only sustainable development will enable us to avert a major environmental and human catastrophe.

However, the word 'sustainable' as used in the Brundtland Report refers nowadays to radically different approaches to development, which result in diametrically opposed economic practices. Increasingly, the word is used by North Americans to mean that development is sustainable for as long as there is a steady supply of resources to sustain it (which implies that resources may be destroyed if deposits of unexploited resources are identified). According to the European approach, on the other hand, development is sustainable only if the known environmental capital is preserved intact.

The term *empowerment*, widely used in the Programme of Action, is another example of imprecision, but of a different sort. In the debate on the status of women it is essentially a polemical expression for forming alliances between interest groups. It summons up unexpressed ideas, ones often not structured by thought, along the lines of 'you see what I mean'. Such imprecision is unacceptable in the Latin languages. Consequently, the French and Spanish translations of this concept are sometimes conventional wordings meaning 'promotion of women', which do not reveal its innovative nature. Stylistic contortions are also used, their sheer variety and awkwardness reflecting the vagueness of the original.

The term empowerment is all the more ambiguous because it is used in a naive sense by the protagonists in the population negotiations. The verb *to empower* first appeared in 1654 with the meaning 'to invest legally or formally with power or authority' (Oxford English Dictionary). It reappeared and became fashionable in the 1980s with a loose meaning as part of the American 'new management' techniques. Their true purpose was to increase company profits by removing as many middle managers as possible. To do that, companies ostensibly gave their executives more responsibility after convincing them of their ability to become real 'managers'. The results of this ploy are well known: most of the executives are now unemployed, and those that remain are being worked to the limits of their physical and psychological endurance.

9

Table 1.3 *Cultural Interpretations of Empowerment*

Original version	French translation	Spanish translation
The *empowerment* of women is a highly important end in itself.	Le *renforcement des moyens d'action* de la femme constitue en soi une fin importante.	La *habilitación* de la mujer es un fin de importancia.
Advancing *empowerment* of women is a cornerstone of population/development programmes.	Assurer la *promotion* des femmes est un élément capital des programmes de population/ développement.	*Promover los derechos* de la mujer es la piedra angular de los programas de población y desarrollo
Gender equality, equity and *empowerment* of women.	Égalité et équité ~~entre~~ les sexes et *promotion* des femmes.	Igualdad, equidad entre los sexos y *habilitación* de la mujer.

These days, empowerment is in disgrace in the business world because the real reasons for it are now clear. Similarly, several of the countries of the South realized the trap lurking in the 'empowerment of women' after asking themselves what it could possibly refer to in societies where the people are powerless.

The Principle of Specificity

'Depending on circumstances' and 'as appropriate' are expressions found in numerous UN recommendations. They are designed to restrict the scope of a recommendation to situations deemed relevant by those responsible for giving effect to it. The Programme of Action on Population and Development makes the specific nature of national situations its guiding principle, although this does not prevent it from making recommendations intended to be universally applicable.

The skilful use of these three principles and the discretionary practice of entering reservations enabled all parties to the negotiations to leave Cairo with a sense of satisfaction, feeling that they had scored points and at the same time contributed to moving the debate forward. Consequently, local-level implementation of an international programme depends essentially on the way the actors concerned interpret it. The strength of an international agreement of this sort lies in its universality. Its weakness lies in the fact that its implementation depends largely on governments' political will and the dynamism of people at the grass roots, because states are not legally obliged to honour their commitments.

The Cairo Conference: Appearance and Reality

The title of the Cairo meeting was 'Conference on Population and Development'. This distinguished it from the two previous UN conferences, whose official title contained the word 'population' but not 'development'. Because the Conference had broader terms of reference, the Programme of Action was generally expected to concentrate on the population aspect of sustainable development and to take further the efforts made in Rio de Janeiro. Unfortunately, however, this expectation was not fulfilled, and development remained the Programme's poor relation.

Preparation of the Conference

Adoption of the Programme of Action was the outcome of a three-year preparatory process involving various categories of participants. It comprised three main stages: technical, regional and international. First of all, experts were approached to discuss various topics. The Conference secretariat had selected six topics: family planning, women, population structure, demographic policies, migration, and the interrelationships between population and environment. Next, conferences were held in Africa, Asia, the Arab countries, Latin America and Europe to discuss region-specific problems. Lastly, there were international meetings of repesentatives of all UN member states. The UN Secretary-General appointed Nafis Sadik, Executive Director of UNFPA, to oversee the preparation of the Conference. She included in her secretariat Population Division and UNFPA officials. The secretariat was responsible for preparing the draft document to be submitted for negotiation, leading the discussions, mobilizing public opinion and helping groups that wished to put forward their views on Conference issues.

Development of the Topics

Each type of meeting produced its own recommendations to be taken into account in preparing the draft programme of action. Figure 1.1 highlights the relative importance accorded to the topics at each stage of the negotiations. It illustrates by means of shading the extent to which each topic appears in the recommendations of the preparatory meetings. At one extreme, white indicates that a topic was not discussed at all, while at the other extreme, black indicates that more than fifty recommendations were devoted to it.

This comparison prompts a number of observations. Generally speaking, family planning and women's issues were discussed at all meetings without exception. Sustainable development and reproductive health were also dealt

11

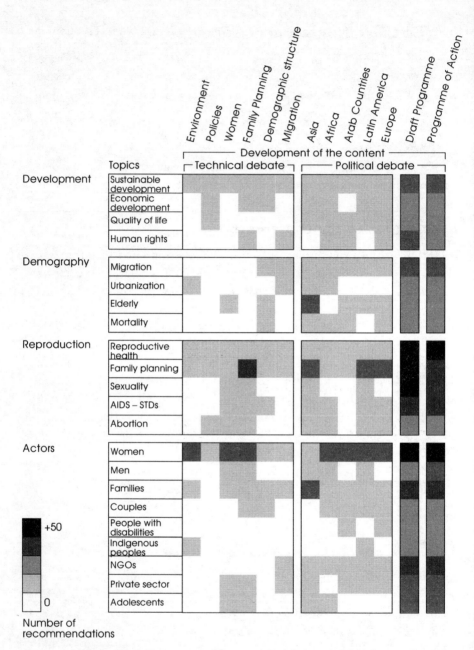

Figure 1.1 *Programme of Action on Population and Development*

with systematically, but much more superficially.

The scientific content of the demographic discussions at the preparatory stage's technical meetings appears to have been very slight. There was very little discussion of standard demographic variables: for example, general mortality was not considered at a meeting of experts, unlike at the 1974 and 1984 conferences. The recommendations of the technical meetings concentrated on reproductive and women's issues.

Similarly, the political stage focused on family planning and women with the exception of the Asian regional conference, whose principal concern was elderly people and the future of the family. The regional conferences did not make recommendations on a number of topics: in Asia, human rights and the concept of the couple; in Africa, elderly people and sexuality; in the Arab countries, economic development, sexuality, abortion and AIDS issues; in Latin America, human rights and adolescents; and in Europe, sexuality, men and adolescents.

There was a considerable lack of continuity between the preparatory stage and the draft programme of action. Of all the topics discussed, reproduction and women received the fullest treatment. Slightly more attention was devoted to sustainable development, human rights, migration and the actors involved (particularly the family and non-governmental organizations), and slightly less to the elderly.

The Conference negotiations changed the draft programme very little. Human rights, family planning and sexuality were placed at a lower level, while men's responsibility for implementing the Programme was placed at a higher level. The few differences between the draft programme and the final text illustrate the fact that although everything was theoretically negotiable up until the Programme's adoption, it was in practice very difficult to amend the document. The cumbersome nature of the process prevented any substantive last-minute restructuring. Consequently, governments endeavoured to agree on the structure and content of the bulk of the document at the international preparatory meetings so that at the Conference itself they had to deal only with the controversial aspects. The practice was therefore not to reopen the debate on those recommendations that had already achieved an informal consensus; in the case of the population programme, this amounted to over 75 per cent of the text. However, a few new elements could still be introduced at the last minute provided that they related to subjects on which consensus had already been achieved in other fora. Accordingly, several recommendations on indigenous peoples and people with disabilities were added.

The Programme of Action on Population and Development runs to 107 pages of recommendations, divided into sixteen chapters. There are three main sets of topics with different levels of concern; each has its own logic and refers to specific issues of social structure and relations among peoples. The first set, the most important one in terms of number of recommendations and political visibility, covers reproduction, women and the family. The second set, which is relatively diluted, is structured around the interrelationships between population dynamics and development. The third set encompasses mortality, migration and the elderly, topics largely avoided or dealt with only superficially and therefore all the more challenging.

A careful reading of the Programme of Action reveals, scattered throughout it, a set of recommendations concerning methods of implementation. Strictly speaking, these are not technical measures; rather, they are a political foundation that gives the whole text a certain tone. The text is marked by the international relations language of the 1990s, the key phrases of which are 'human rights', 'political transparency' and 'partnership with civil society'. Chapters 2–5 review those topics and recommendations, identifying progress made in the negotiations as well as shortcomings and sticking points. Whatever happened, however, certainly did not dampen the enthusiasm of the negotiators. As a European diplomat said on his arrival in Cairo, 'Whether the negotiations succeed or fail, the Conference will be a success!'

Chapter 2

A Life of Quality

Reproduction, Women and the Family: Programme of Action

The recommendations on reproduction, women and the family cover five main areas:

1. reproduction, reproductive rights, health problems and sexuality;
2. family planning, freedom of choice and contraceptive services;
3. the family, its social function and protection, and relations among its members;
4. the Programme's main target groups; and
5. those responsible for implementing the recommendations.

The recommendations are summarized below.

Reproductive Health

Reproductive rights embrace certain human rights that are already recognized in national laws, international human rights documents and other United Nations consensus documents. Everyone has the right to enjoy the highest attainable standard of physical and mental health, including in the areas of sexuality and reproduction. All couples and individuals have the right to decide freely and responsibly the number and spacing of their children, and to have the information, education and means to do so, free of discrimination, coercion and violence. This right also applies to people with disabilities. In exercising their reproductive rights, couples and individuals should take into account their responsibilities towards the community, and the needs of their existing and future children.

Every country must have a proper primary health care system. If necessary, the state must overhaul its health system in order to streamline the allocation of resources. The management of reproductive health programmes must be decentralized and undertaken in partnership with non-governmental organizations and the private sector. Governments should include reproductive health services in primary health care. Programmes should be geared to the groups for which they are intended so as to take account of their specific characteristics and needs. Scientific studies should be made of men's and women's perceived birth control and sexual health needs. Similarly, research should help to determine why existing services are not used.

Reproductive health services encompass child health, safe motherhood, infant survival, family planning, prenatal care and advice, safe delivery, postnatal care and advice, and sexual health. Programmes must monitor dangerous pregnancies, prevent sexually transmitted diseases and malnutrition, and maternal and child diseases; provide information about family planning, sexuality and infant care; and make available contraceptive means. Sexual health implies that an individual can have a safe and satisfying sex life, and its aim is to improve the quality of life and interpersonal relationships. It thus extends beyond counselling and care related to reproduction and sexually transmitted diseases.

The fundamental causes of maternal mortality should be identified and it must be reduced by 50 per cent by the year 2000, and again by 50 per cent between 2000 and 2015. Reproductive health and family planning services should be accessible to all individuals of appropriate age no later than the year 2015.

Full exercise of reproductive choice requires a number of conditions to be in place. The four main ones are:

1. a wide range of services which an individual may use without being pressured;
2. adequate knowledge of the contraceptive choices available;
3. an appropriate climate, free from any form of coercion, which respects the privacy of the individual and permits a democratic public debate; and
4. respect for the diversity of situations and the power relations involved.

To achieve those conditions, it is therefore important to ensure that everyone has the ability to choose, particularly the most vulnerable groups and individuals. There must also be respect for differences between cultures, genders and age groups, as well as for disabilities.

The AIDS pandemic must be combated in such a way as to harmonize with the perceptions of local health priorities. To combat sexually transmitted diseases, it is necessary to develop information, education and communication programmes advocating responsible sexual behaviour; to integrate prevention, detection and care provision in reproductive health and family planning programmes; to monitor the quality of blood products; to increase investment in medical research aimed at developing an AIDS vaccine and self-protection for women; to carry out socioeconomic studies to improve understanding of spread factors; and to care for AIDS victims, releasing additional funds for treating HIV-positive patients and looking after orphans.

High-risk sexual behaviour, sexual mutilation of women, incest and various forms of sexual violence involving major health risks must be eliminated, together with trafficking for the purposes of prostitution. Sexual harassment should be banned, and labour legislation amended to that end.

Information, education and communication strategies should be interlinked so as to supplement reproductive health services, to increase their use and to improve the quality of care. Sociocultural studies should make awareness and information programmes acceptable, effective and useful. To that end, governments must base their policies on a better understanding of actual sexual behaviour. Information and education play a leading role in promoting responsible sexual behaviour. Sex education should begin at home and at school. Men and young boys must be made aware of, and educated in, their sexual and reproductive responsibilities.

Campaigns should be conducted among all types of local, community, religious and political authorities in order to make them aware of the harmful effects of sexual mutilation on girls' and women's health.

Abortion

In no case should abortion be promoted as a method of family planning. Governments, as well as intergovernmental and non-governmental organizations, are urged to deal with the health impact of unsafe abortion as a major public health concern and to reduce the recourse to abortion through expanded and improved family-planning services. Every attempt should be made to eliminate the need for abortion. In circumstances where abortion is not against the law, such abortion should be safe. Women should have access to quality services for the management of complications arising from abortion. Post-abortion counselling, education and family-planning services should be offered promptly to avoid repeat abortions.

Family Planning

The aim of family planning is to enable couples and individuals to prevent unwanted and high-risk pregnancies. All countries should make quality family-planning services affordable, acceptable and accessible to those who need and want them, while maintaining confidentiality. Programmes should offer a wide range of services without any form of coercion. Governments must replace incentive- and disincentive-based strategies by measures focusing on increased education and voluntary measures. Systems to monitor and evaluate family-planning programmes should make it possible to ensure that services are consistent with human rights and ethical and professional standards.

Informed free choice is essential to the long-term success of family-planning programmes. Governments and the international community are urged to use all means at their disposal to support the principle of voluntary choice in family planning. Family planning must be carried out within certain limits: the limits laid down by law; the constraints inherent in each individual's potential (everyone has the right to the enjoyment of the highest attainable standard of physical and mental health); and the constraints imposed by respect for one's partner and by children's needs. The principle of choice is also closely linked to the principle of responsibility that must underpin it: the responsibility of governments for establishing adequate policies, programmes and services; the responsibility of the various social players (non-governmental organizations, the private sector), and the individual's responsibility towards society.

Services must be accessible to everyone, particularly the most underserved and vulnerable groups. They must focus primarily on the needs of women and adolescents, groups that should be involved in preparing, implementing and following up programmes. These programmes must reach men in the workplace, at home and where they gather for recreation. Improving the quality of services is a cornerstone of the Programme of Action. Substantial progress must be made in five areas: promoting a wide choice of both modern and traditional methods, particularly breastfeeding, which promotes the spacing of births and child survival; improving information about family-planning methods, their effectiveness, risks and side effects; improving the supply of contraceptives; improving staff training, particularly in the detection of sexually transmitted diseases, care, programme management and relations with patients; and ensuring better monitoring of individuals using contraceptive methods and improved evaluation of programme operation.

Over the next several years, all countries should evaluate their family-planning needs and identify obstacles to the use of family-planning services. Governments and the international community should use all means at their disposal to defend publicly, steadfastly and firmly the delivery and use of family-planning services. Their objective should be to overcome obstacles to family planning by the year 2005. Governments should abolish all forms of restrictions hampering individuals' and couples' use of contraception, and meet all currently unmet needs by 2015.

Scientific research must help to increase the range of available choices through improvement of birth-control methods and development of new, easy methods of use. It is necessary to carry out studies of men's and women's perceived contraceptive and sexual health service needs, as well as of the reasons why existing techniques and services are not used. The new birth-control methods must be appropriate for individuals, and different cultures and age groups.

The Family

The family is the basic unit of society. Marriage must be entered into with the free consent of the intending spouses; child marriage should be abolished. Parents must assume their financial obligations towards their children. Those persons with authority in the family must speak out and act forcefully against a preference for sons.

Governments should ensure that laws and policies promote the maintenance or reconstitution of the family unit, and should make every effort to assist the building of family-like ties in especially difficult circumstances, for example those involving street children. Governments are urged to recognize the vital importance of the family group and to take measures to ensure the protection and normalization of the family life of migrants.

The family must be protected and supported, particularly those families weakened by an economically precarious situation, migration, conflicts and catastrophes. Governments must create an appropriate environment for the family through the adoption of appropriate sectoral policies, particularly in housing, social security, health and education, and they must evaluate the impact of such policies on the family.

Governments must encourage multigenerational families. Social security measures must address those social, cultural and economic factors behind the increasing costs of child-rearing. The earning opportunities of all adult members of economically deprived families must be increased through job programmes. All necessary measures must be taken to enable parents to combine labour force participation with parental responsibilities, especially single-parent families. Vulnerable families must be the subject of special support measures – for example, families with sociopsychological problems, such as alcoholism, domestic violence, drug addiction, incest and abandoned children – as well as families victimized by famine, wars and racial violence. Minimum-wage allowances should be paid to needy single parents with dependants. Assistance should be provided to persons with disabilities to enable them to exercise their rights and fulfil their family responsibilities.

The traditional gender-based division of parental and domestic functions does not reflect current realities and aspirations. In all parts of the world, a growing number of women are in paid employment outside the home. Consequently, men and women should establish a genuine partnership and share family tasks, the tasks of working life, and child care and rearing. Women and men should be able to take parental leave. Awareness campaigns must encourage men's equal sharing in household tasks and in all family responsibilities. Laws should be amended to compel men to assume their family responsibilities, and legal measures should oblige them to pay the necessary allowances. Relationships based on equality and mutual respect must be established between men and women, as well as mutual consideration and willingness to accept the consequences of a sexual relationship.

In order to elaborate and monitor these policies and programmes, governments should strengthen machinery for monitoring changes in family structure and composition, especially in respect of single-parent and multigenerational families.

Women

The human rights of women and the girl child are an inalienable, integral and indivisible part of universal human rights. Women should enjoy the right equally with men to buy, hold and sell property and land; to obtain credit and negotiate contracts in their own name and on their own behalf; and to exercise their legal rights to inherit.

Legal obstacles to women's full participation in political and public life must be removed. They must be involved in policy- and decision-making processes at all stages, and in all areas of development. All forms of discriminatory practices by employers against women must eliminated, such as with regard to recruitment (particularly the requirement of proof of contraceptive use and pregnancy status), income, access to social security systems and employment security. Various measures should be taken to enable women to combine the roles of child-bearing, breastfeeding and child-rearing with participation in the workforce, including the provision of health insurance and social security, day-care centres, workplace breastfeeding facilities and creches, part-time employment, paid parental leave and flexible working hours.

Women should participate in the elaboration and implementation of women-related programmes. They must receive an education that enables them to meet their basic needs and exercise their rights. Machinery must be established to foster their participation and enable them to articulate their concerns and needs. Specific procedures and indicators should be devised for gender-based analysis of development programmes and for assessing their impact on women's social, economic and health status and access to resources. Women should have equal work opportunities with men; they must be able to achieve economic self-reliance and earn income beyond traditional occupations.

Adolescents

Adolescents have specific reproductive health needs. Parents and other persons legally responsible for adolescents have a duty and responsibility to guide them. Countries must ensure that adolescents have access to the necessary information and services, particularly with regard to sexual abuse and sexually transmitted diseases.

Adolescents have the right to privacy, confidentiality and dignity. Those countries that have laws or impose social restrictions preventing adolescents from receiving information about reproductive health services and using them should abolish such provisions. Adolescents must be involved in planning services relevant to them. All those persons who are in a position to provide guidance to adolescents concerning responsible sexual behaviour should receive appropriate training.

Children

Children are the most important resource. The state and the family must give them the highest possible priority. Child mortality is governed by many factors: poverty, malnutrition, a decline in breastfeeding, inadequacy or lack of sanitation and of health facilities, civil unrest and wars, unwanted births, ill treatment and AIDS. Infant and under-5 child mortality must be reduced by one-third before the year 2000, or to 50 and 70 per 1000 live births respectively. Excess mortality among girl infants and children must be eliminated.

Parents and societies must invest as much as possible in children so as to develop their capabilities. They must be protected by legislative, administrative, social and educational measures from all forms of physical or mental violence, injury or abuse, maltreatment and exploitation, trafficking in organs and sexual abuse. Governments must establish the necessary conditions and procedures to encourage children to report violations of their human rights, and must ban the production of and trade in child pornography. Countries must adopt collective measures to alleviate the suffering of children in armed conflicts and natural disasters. Governments must facilitate the integration of migrants' children through education, training and naturalization.

Countries must give priority to the survival, protection and development of children, and make every effort to combat neglect and abandonment. They must find solutions to the problems of street children and set up care centres and special protection and rehabilitation programmes. Safe motherhood, child survival and family planning services, together with their specific components (health education, postnatal care, food supplements and promotion of breastfeeding), should be complemented by child care education for parents.

Non-Governmental Organizations, the Private Sector and Community Groups

Participation by non-governmental organizations must be regarded as supplementing government action in the provision of reproductive and sexual health services and family-planning services. Non-governmental organizations must mobilize family and community support, and make sexual health and family planning services more accessible and acceptable. Women's organizations in particular should be involved in the decision-making process. Governments and donor countries must ensure that the autonomy of non-governmental organizations is protected.

The private, profit-oriented sector has an important role to play, particularly in the production of contraceptives and the delivery of reproductive health services. It must engage in information and education activities in a socially responsible, culturally sensitive and cost-effective manner.

To carry out their information and awareness programmes successfully, governments should mobilize all social groups (non-governmental organizations, religious authorities, the private sector, media, schools, health services), although action in the first instance must be family- and community-based.

When the state of government thinking before the Cairo Conference is borne in mind, the Programme of Action can be said to have taken three significant steps forward. First, it introduced a new concept – 'reproductive health' – which is more comprehensive than family planning. Second, it recognized sexuality as a fundamental aspect of human existence, but also one fraught

21

with problems. Third, it took account of women as persons fully responsible for their own choices, to whom reproduction-related programmes are of the greatest relevance.

A New Concept: Reproductive Health

The term *reproductive health* refers to a state of complete physical, mental and social well-being in all matters relating to the reproductive system and processes. It extends beyond the absence of disease and infirmity and therefore implies sexual health, i.e. the possibility of having a satisfying and safe sex life, the capability to reproduce and the freedom to decide if, when and how often to do so. Reproductive health services encompass the full range of methods and techniques required for that purpose. Reproductive health recognizes other individual needs, and not solely unmet contraceptive needs. It extends beyond the technical side of family planning, since it takes into account the factors affecting reproductive behaviour. These include the role of men, power relations between the sexes, the status of women, and the role of social institutions in reproductive strategies and individual choices. Implementation of the concept endeavours to integrate the viewpoint of women as persons with specific health needs.

The concept of reproductive health is relatively new, and came into being after doubts had been expressed about family planning programmes centred on the regulation of fertility and the supply of contraceptives. Various factors helped to widen the perspective of family planning programmes. Major national and international surveys during the 1980s highlighted the interrelationships between the spacing of births and infants' and mothers' chances of survival. During the same period attempts to control sexually transmitted diseases and, more recently, the AIDS epidemic created an awareness of sexuality's leading role in people's general state of health. Scientists, women's groups and bodies such as the Ford Foundation, the International Women's Health Coalition, the World Health Organization and the Population Council played a major role in setting out an integrated approach to reproduction, which was termed *reproductive health*. The Cairo Conference was an important step in legitimizing this concept.

As Carla Makhlouf emphasizes, the advantage of this concept in practical terms is that it is based on various vague categories which give it the flexibility to take account of different groups' concerns. It is more a consensus-oriented idea than a standard-setting definition stipulating how programmes are to be structured. Accordingly, implementing reproductive health programmes essentially means taking account of the diverse and specific nature of the needs of all women: migrant women, women in countries with economies in transition, single women and women of all ages. It also means enabling women to participate in all stages of these programmes' elaboration and implementation, as both actors and beneficiaries.

Against this background, the Programme of Action implicitly recognizes the abuses and distortions to which family planning programmes and biomedical research may be subject. It recommends that these be publicly identified and averted through the adoption of strict criteria and scientific standards in fertility regulation research, and through the establishment of national bodies to assess the ethics of contraception. In addition, the Programme acknowledges that non-medical contraceptive methods can be effective and useful, and therefore advocates equal support for research into natural family-planning methods.

Abortion was undoubtedly the most controversial issue at the Cairo Conference, so much so that some sections of the public thought it was a conference on abortion. It is hardly a new issue, however. As long ago as the 1974 Bucharest Conference, governments acknowledged the impact of illegal abortions on female morbidity and mortality. At the Mexico City Conference in 1984, they laid down the principle that abortion should not be promoted as a contraceptive method, and at the same time reaffirmed the need to help women avoid having recourse to it and to give appropriate assistance to those who had had abortions. After much debate, the Cairo Conference produced a recommendation that repeated the previous positions – in other words, abortion should be regarded as a 'public health problem'. What was new, however, was the recommendation that legal abortions be safe. This is because in many countries where abortions are legal, for various reasons they are not always carried out under proper medical conditions.

Table 2.1 *Abortion*

Conference	Recommendation
Bucharest, 1974	The number of illegal abortions should be reduced as part of the efforts to reduce morbidity and mortality.
Mexico City, 1984	As part of the efforts to reduce morbidity and mortality, governments must help women to avoid abortion, which under no circumstances should be promoted as a family planning method. As far as possible, they should extend humane treatment to women who have had an abortion and should provide them with counselling.
Cairo, 1994	In circumstances where abortion is not against the law, such abortion should be safe.

Available data suggest that unsafe abortions are a major cause of maternal mortality and morbidity, and therefore pose a real health problem. Although far from comprehensive, the data reveal that 40–60 million abortions are performed every year, one in four pregnancies being terminated. More than half of these abortions are illegal and are not carried out under proper medical conditions.

Recognition of Sexuality

The concept of reproductive health is founded upon the recognition that reproduction is grounded in a basic fact, one which is the source of our existence as a species – namely, sexuality.

> 'The fact that human sexual reproduction results in a diversity of individuals is rarely accepted for what it is: one of the mainsprings of evolution, a natural phenomenon without which we would not belong to this world. More often than not, this diversity is regarded as scandalous by those who criticize the social order and wish to make all individuals the same. Or it is seen as a means of oppression by those who seek to justify the social order in terms of an allegedly natural order, one to which they assign all individuals on the basis of the norm, i.e. themselves.'[1]

In daring to address the reproduction issue so radically, the Cairo Conference not only broke a long-standing taboo, but also raised many problems that had hitherto received scant attention – for example, sexual mutilation, to which two million women are subjected every year. The Conference viewed sexuality as a dimension of well-being and an important aspect of interpersonal relationships. Among the problems raised were the exploitation of women, the regulation of fertility and the relationships between the health aspects of reproduction and sexually transmitted diseases, including AIDS. By discussing these issues in detail, the Conference affirmed not only that sexuality exists, but also that it can cause problems, often affecting mainly women.

Sexual Behaviours and Contraception

The diversity of sexual behaviours and of the values associated with them impacts on contraceptive choices. For that reason, the Programme of Action refers to the need for a proper understanding of the relationships between sexual behaviours and people's contraceptive needs so that family planning services can be geared to individual experience. When sexuality is taken into account, it becomes clear that neither reproductive health should be separated from sexual health, nor contraception from prevention and treatment of sexually transmitted diseases. In practical terms, this new approach involves training family-planning programme personnel to take account of the sexual aspect of health and behavioural problems.

In considering not only the health aspects of sexuality but also the interpersonal and social aspects, the Programme of Action identifies various gender inequities deriving from the realities of sexuality. It also gives currency to the view that men tend to behave irresponsibly in sexual matters and that women alone have to suffer the consequences. Not only is this generalization dangerous, but also it is contradicted by various examples of countries or periods in which it fell to men – not women – to decide to use contraceptive methods.[2]

Sexual Health

The extent of women's sufferings, especially in countries with an inadequate health system, has long been underestimated. The Cairo Programme of Action was the first population programme to recognize the health problems caused by sexual mutilation and their lasting impact on women from the reproductive and psychological point of view. Surveys have progressively revealed the extent of suffering caused by gynaecological problems. A recent two-year study of a group of women from two African villages[3] revealed, for example, that 85 per cent of them had a gynaecological problem. Although 64 per cent had suspicious symptoms, only 13 per cent believed that this was not 'normal', and only a third intended to see a doctor. Most of the time, the women dare not mention their sufferings and accept them as part of their lives. Family-planning services are frequently inadequate for such women because they are designed for healthy women.

Adolescent Sexuality

Adolescent sexuality is still difficult to discuss, particularly since the generation gap is widening. Teenage pregnancy statistics and the spread of AIDS testify to the problem of young people's sexual activities. Surveys show that the problem is both universal and diverse, its many different forms depending on culture, ethnic group, social level and the circumstances at a particular time. If adolescents' needs are to be met, the approach adopted must take account of this diversity.

The Female Perspective

Autonomy, *empowerment* and *gender* are key words for understanding a programme of action that attaches great importance to women's needs and perspectives. It lists and condemns all forms of violence against women: rape in war time, trafficking in women, pornography, prenatal sex selection and sexual harassment. It reiterates and expands on what was said at the Bucharest and Mexico City conferences about women's education, employment, equality and discrimination, and the combining of parental, family and work roles. It emphasizes women's work burden and the better use they could make of their time if they were able to do so. Women's groups are encouraged in their consciousness-raising efforts. The various types of inequality are detailed, especially those stemming from discriminatory practices, abuse of power and denial of rights. The Programme recommends new indicators and procedures to assess respect for the principle of equality, including in the enforcement of laws prohibiting forced marriages.

Discrimination from Birth

The Programme of Action is founded upon the implicit assertion that being a woman is a disadvantage from birth, one that must be remedied by altering legislative bias, changing behaviour and overhauling the way in which institutions operate. Even before they are born, girls often have less chance of survival than boys because of sex selection, infanticide, or insufficient food and health care. Of course, some progress has been made and current generations are better off, but such progress is still very scanty in many fields and, in particular, unevenly spread throughout the world. Furthermore, this progress is not necessarily irreversible.

In 24 industrialized nations studied by Tabutin, the excess mortality of girls aged from 5 to 15 years old was a widespread phenomenon between 1800 and 1940. It started gradually to disappear at the beginning of this century because of the rapid decline in infectious and parasitic diseases and the simultaneous rise in male excess mortality (due to accidents and violence); the increase in regular schooling; the development of the health system; the legal regulation of labour (i.e. minimum working age and hours); the legal protection of women and children; the emergence of the 'modern' family with its new attitude towards women and children; the decline in fertility; and women's new aspirations for themselves and their children.[4]

Lack of Education

Education was the second basic factor in women's inequality highlighted in the Programme of Action. One of the consequences of the scant importance attached to women's lives and the belief that their place is in the home is that they receive less education than men. Of the approximately 960 million illiterate adults in the world, two-thirds are women; and of the 130 million children who do not go to school, 70 per cent are girls. Equality in schooling for girls and boys is therefore a priority. Nevertheless, it should be borne in mind, as Hervé Le Bras points out, that compulsory schooling is not acceptable unless it offers prospects for advancement: 'It is development that leads to a demand for education, more so than vice versa...acceptance of mass education requires very cogent religious or economic reasons'.[5] In his view, primary school education alone will not have a profound effect on girls' future lives; what is essential is secondary school education, i.e. education during puberty.

Overburdened with Work but Without Paid Employment

One of the principles set out in the Programme of Action is that women's employment outside the home is not only an increasingly common phenomenon but is also a prerequisite for improving their lot. Women's ability to enter the workforce depends on at least three closely related factors – education, social status and cultural environment. It also depends on the economic circumstances prevailing at a particular time. Generally speaking, women are a secondary labour force: they are the first to be dismissed and a greater number proportionately than men work part time. They are required to furnish proof that they are not pregnant and to undertake that they do not intend to fall pregnant in the near future. In a number of countries, laws and customs prohibit women from inheriting property or land or obtaining credit. Frequently they do not earn the same as men for work requiring the same educational background, even though equal pay may be a legal requirement.

Regardless of their integration and the length of time spent working outside the home, women's workload exceeds that of men everywhere except in North America and Australia. In seventeen countries of the South, women work about 30 per cent more than men every day. One reason for this is that they do farm work in addition to performing their domestic and child-rearing duties.

The concept of gender permeates the Programme of Action. Whereas the term 'empowerment' is essentially a slogan, 'gender' started life as a category in sociological analysis. Unfortunately, however, since abstractions are not at home in international negotiations, frequent use of this word in the international women's debate has started a fruitless argument based on a

In the news

She's 13 and Already Married

There is no one law governing the rights of Palestinian women or the minimum legal age for marriage. Egyptian law is still in force in the Gaza Strip, while Jordanian law applies in the West Bank and Israeli law in East Jerusalem. Thanks to this legislative anarchy, girls are commonly married off at the age of 13 or 14... According to Roukia Omar, a teacher, 'every class in our school has a number of brides. I try to encourage my pupils to get themselves an education, which is a weapon for women, but family pressure carries the day... We have no upper school. We started a class at that level ... but we did not have enough pupils: most of them were already married...'. According to Sheikh Mohamed Abou Sardanat, an Islamic court judge, 'it is not the laws that are anarchic but their enforcement... We are trying to set up joint committees in the West Bank and the Gaza Strip to standardize legislation, but this requires patience. Islam, it should be noted, is fair to women. A girl who marries early is still only a child and does not understand the meaning of marriage. We use the wise advice of our religion to remedy that problem'.

Majida al-Batch, Al Quds Al-Arabi, *March 1995, London*

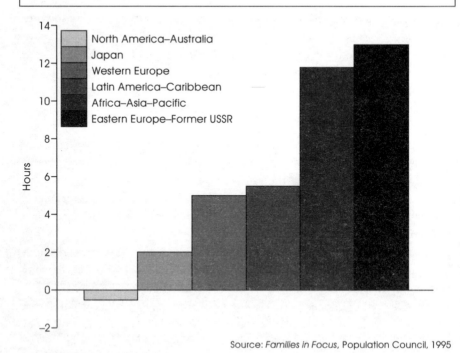

Source: *Families in Focus*, Population Council, 1995

Figure 2.1 *Difference Between the Number of Hours Worked per Day by Men and Women*

28

Table 2.2 *Cultural Interpretations of Gender*

Original text	French translation	Spanish translation
Leaders must speak against *gender* discrimination.	Les personnes ayant de l'autorité doivent s'élever contre les *comportements discriminatoires.*	Los dirigentes deverian manifestarse en contra de las formas de *discrimin-ación por razones de sexo.*
School curricula must eliminate *gender bias.*	Le contenu des programmes doit éliminer tout parti pris *sexiste.*	Los planes de estudios deben eliminar todas las formas de *discriminación basada en el sexo.*
Countries should train teachers to be more *gender* sensitive.	Les pays devraient sensibiliser les enseignants aux *disparités entre les sexes.*	...para que los maestros sean más sensibles a los *problemas de las mujeres.*

misunderstanding of its meaning and scope. In Cairo, a number of delegations thought that feminists were using this term to justify the existence of a third sex – neuter – additional to the two biologically recognized ones. Therefore they wasted their time, energy and money on what was in fact a non-debate. However, it is important not to underestimate the considerable cultural differences underlying the meaning attributed to this originally Anglo-Saxon concept (see Table 2.2). In the Romance languages, for example, 'gender' essentially refers to the difference between the two sexes. Consequently, it may be wondered whether this word is not perchance a *sociologically correct* way of referring to sex!

The Origin of 'Gender'
Anne Zwahlen

The concept of gender first appeared – in the US – during the 1970s in feminist research in the social and historical sciences. After an initial period of almost exclusively female-oriented research, an attempt was made to analyse social relationships between men and women so as to highlight the structural causes of women's generally inferior status. The concept is threefold. First, biological sex is differentiated from social sex: apart from men's fertilization capability and women's child-bearing capability, everything is gender, i.e. everything is a social construct that can be changed and renegotiated. Second, gender highlights the point at which the notions of feminine and masculine meet by revealing the asymmetries, hierarchies and different valuations of each one. Third, gender is claimed to be a cross-disciplinary view of social issues, a principle that structures the world seen in its material and symbolic organization.

In 1985, the International Development Institute at Harvard University developed the first gender analysis framework for development programmes. It has four elements: the general context's differential influence on men and women; the sexual division of labour; access to resources; and decision-making machinery. Gender analysis is particularly used to study male–female differences in the division of labour and access to resources. The Harvard model fostered discussion of a neglected aspect of social reality. However, it attracted a number of criticisms, two of which are significant. First, because it concentrated on microsocial matters – the family, the couple and the man–woman relationship – gender analysis was seen as being marred by ethnocentrism. Second, those experts carrying out observation and analysis were not part of the environment they were studying, and there was no input from the persons actually involved.

Other models have been developed from the Harvard model. One of these is Caroline Moser's model, based on the dynamics between women's practical needs (actual living conditions) and strategic interests. Caroline Moser defines those interests, using as a basis the inequality and the power relations between men and women. In her view, development programmes are on the wrong track in seeking to meet women's needs rather than endeavouring to serve their strategic interests. Thus they fail to take account of the power phenomena underlying all social change.

The Swiss overseas development and cooperation agency (DDC) has created its own gender analysis framework for development programmes. It is in fact more than a framework: it is an interactive and participatory approach designed to evolve in accordance with local dynamics. The assumption is that those who have recourse to the framework in their work are fully aware of their own gender relationships and those inherent in their particular organization. These persons must be able to distinguish the levels at which gender relationships are likely to arise: family groups, communities or state bodies.

The analysis comprises six major elements:

1. identifying the social imagination, values and mechanisms by which male and female stereotypes are formed;
2. taking account of the status of individuals, especially women, in social and family structure;
3. considering diversity within groups, among both men and women;
4. studying the sexual division of labour, duties and responsibilities, as well as women's various roles;
5. identifying the means of access to resources, and resource monitoring and differentiated use; and
6. assessing the impact of the general situation (political, economic, legal, social and cultural aspects) on men and women.

In practical terms, gender analysis should help reveal inequalities in access to resources and in the apportionment of tasks. It should also offer ways of maintaining solidarity between men and women, so as to enable them to negotiate a different division of tasks and found their relationships upon a new and mutually beneficial balance.

In the news

Czech Feminism

The word 'feminism' automatically conjures up in this country the image of the radical wing of the American women's movement.Women who march in the streets waving their bras. Feminists who refuse to procreate.Young women who accuse men of sexual harassment before the men have even dared glance in their direction. Consequently, it is not surprising that most organizations here do not want to be labelled feminist...

There are more than thirty women's organizations in our country... Christian women, women company bosses, women research scientists and lesbians all have their own organizations. Some movements, such as the Mothers of Prague or their equivalent in southern Bohemia, are ecological. Just about the only avowedly feminist organization is New Humankind... Unlike their colleagues in the West, most of the leading figures in the Czech feminist movement are married with children. Their outlook is more or less as follows: if women threw themselves more boldly into public life and working life, they would exert a civilizing and humanizing influence on a society hitherto shaped largely by male attitudes. They could use their more finely tuned sensibilities for solving educational, health and social problems... Women's organizations aim to achieve their objectives through long-term work among women, offering them educational activities and self-assertion courses. They are not declaring war on men: that would be playing them at their own game.

Lidové Noviny, February 1995, Prague

Many aspects of reproduction, women's lives and changing family relationships are not dealt with in the Programme of Action. This is either because they are indicative of the diverse behaviours and complex realities which a universally oriented programme cannot encompass, or because political decision-makers are not yet aware of their importance. As far as the Programme of Action's implementation is concerned, some of these matters deserve greater attention. They include the new difficulties with reproductive patterns, the role of medicalized contraception in relation to the other aspects of birth control, the concept of freedom of choice, the interrelationships between women's work and family well-being, and the changes in family types compared with changes in society.

Claudine Sauvain-Dugerdil stresses in her contribution the importance of not discussing reproduction as an isolated event in women's lives. She emphasizes that motherhood is determined in the first place by the path of a woman's life, her values, and her emotional and socioeconomic circumstances. In addition, she points out that fertility regulation is not new: fertility in Western

American Feminism has Lost its Soul

In the view of most Americans, who believe women have unprecedented freedom and opportunities, feminist talk about the rape culture in which we supposedly live or about the eternal struggle against male oppression paints a picture unrecognizable to most women... Nowadays, we have homosexual feminism, separatist feminism, ecofeminism, anti-abortion feminism. There are vegetarian feminists and feminists who cannot stand perfume... Most black women say – and rightly so – that white feminism does not speak for them. And many Hispanic-American women and Asian-American women do not think it speaks for them either... Despite these divisions, an 'official' feminist movement still speaks out on behalf of women in general... The privileged woman in the feminist movement is a young white professional woman, with a university education and a good income. Consequently, it is her interests that are going to dictate the official movement's priorities: abortion, sexual freedom, easy divorce, tax deductions for domestic help and baby sitters, family leave instead of maternity leave. The feminist hero earns a better living than the average man and, of course, the average woman. But she is not representative of most women.

Elizabeth Fox-Genovese, Le Monde, *March 1995, Paris*

countries declined in circumstances very different from those currently prevailing in the countries of the South. Although acknowledging the importance of contraception in reducing the uncertainty of reproductive patterns, she draws attention to the risks posed by excessively medicalized contraceptive methods and to the perhaps exaggerated importance which the Programme of Action accords contraception compared with other essential birth control factors.

Fertility Control and Reproductive and Life Patterns
Claudine Sauvain-Dugerdil

There are some 500 000 pregnancy-related deaths each year, 99 per cent of them in the countries of the South. The risk of such a death is about one in ten thousand in the industrialized regions of the world, one in twenty in the countries of the South as a whole and one in fifteen in Africa. Long underestimated, the problem was finally acknowledged at the beginning of the 1980s, whereupon the World Health Organization (WHO) and the international community began to develop 'safe motherhood' programmes. In its assessment of the problem, the Cairo Conference's Programme of Action advocates action to ensure the best possible health for the mother and her newborn child, and sets out the services required. It also stresses the prevention of high-risk pregnancies and the need to identify their causes.

Although it devotes twice as much space to family planning as to motherhood-related problems, the Programme of Action hardly ever mentions the causes of high-risk pregnancies, i.e. the vicious circle of malnutrition, insufficient growth, overwork, and fertility-related cultural pressure to produce a male child. Similarly, there is no emphasis on the fundamental importance of first-time pregnancy and the attention it should therefore be accorded.

Motherhood is viewed more as an isolated event than as an aspect of a woman's life history. Consequently, much greater attention is paid to the immediate causes of pregnancy-related deaths – for example, unsatisfactory conditions during pregnancy and childbirth – than to the cumulative effect of adverse elements dating from childhood. The new concept of reproductive health, in the sense of lifelong well-being, requires genuine preventive work to identify not single risk factors but at-risk life patterns. It is clear, however, that pregnancy is in itself a risk factor in women's lives and that birth may involve serious complications. Action to combat maternal mortality therefore requires, among other things, a system to deal with emergencies as they arise, i.e. proper infrastructures, training and information.

Giving life and ensuring that its potential may be properly fulfilled in a human being who contributes to perpetuating his or her group constitute a process deriving from a complex mixture of constraints, chance and choices that have as much to do with a person's innermost being as with the concerns of national policies. The reproductive pattern is a facet of the life pattern an individual constructs and alters throughout his or her existence on the basis of constraints, circumstances and the amount of freedom available. Each individual belongs to a society, a culture and a family whose features are the result of the chance events in a long history of successive generations in a constantly changing environment. Consequently, an individual's life pattern cannot be reduced to mere causality, and it is not surprising that the many models explaining fertility in terms of a juxtaposition of determinants have failed to elucidate the mysteries of reproductive behaviour. Nor is it surprising, as pointed out in the Programme of Action, that many governments' economic and social efforts over the last hundred years to increase or reduce fertility have had only a limited effect.

Children's Needs

The Programme of Action sets out reproductive responsibility not only in terms of the need for a child as experienced by an adult but also in terms of the child's needs. The child's foremost need is naturally the ante- and postnatal care required to ensure his or her survival. Although infant and juvenile mortality has universally decreased since 1960, the persisting worldwide differences in mortality rates reveal the magnitude of the inequalities that remain.

More than merely surviving, children must be able to develop those qualities that will make them responsible human beings capable of fulfilling their role in society. All too often, however, the basic well-being and security to enable them to achieve their potential do not exist, and in some cases the right to satisfy the need to become a mother or father may conflict with the unborn child's rights. There are also cases where a child's needs would be better served in a household other than that of the biological parents. In that connection, it is interesting to note the very flexible system which exists in many traditional societies whereby a child lives temporarily or permanently under a different roof, depending on the needs of society and the family. Moving children from one home to another[6] makes it possible to redistribute human resources and child-related costs within a particular group. Such a situation and the situation of reconstituted families, and other cases in which a child is not reared solely by the parents, raise the issue of the significance of filial ties. How should the 'real' (i.e. genetic) father and the 'real' mother be defined? Should the genetic link be considered supreme, as generally happens in Western societies? Like the Catholic church, should we regard donor-based artificial insemination and fertilization techniques as *impairing the right of the child to be born of a father and mother known to him or her ?*[7] Will a child be happier and better able to fulfil itself if it knows the name of the man whose donation of sperm enabled it to be born? And should the anonymity clause regarding the donor's identity be abolished, as is proposed in Sweden? Is there not a tendency to forget that what counts most are the emotional bonds through which the values that give life a meaning are passed on, and that adoptive motherhood can basically be of the same quality as biological motherhood?[8]

Fertility Regulation

Throughout history, women's 'terrifying' power over life has been surrounded by rituals and subject to controls in accordance with the belief that it is better to procreate sparingly, like the elephant, than like the mango tree buckling under the weight of its own fruit.[9] Those populations known for their particularly high fertility rate have fallen far short of producing the maximum number of children that could be borne if women gave birth annually from the age of 15 to 50. It is estimated that among populations with so-called natural fertility – that is, those that do not deliberately use birth control methods – each woman could bear 15 children if she remained married throughout the whole period of her fertility and did not experience the contraceptive effect of breastfeeding. Those women members of the Hutterite religious community who married before the age of twenty in the 1920s, or Quebec women who married during the first quarter of the eighteenth century, bore an average of approximately eleven children each. However, these examples quoted in demographic literature as the maximum average recorded are still relatively uncommon. Among present-day populations with 'natural' fertility, the average recorded number of children per woman is about six.[10]

Although a clear distinction should be drawn between natural fertility and maximum fertility, it is important to be aware that natural fertility as such does not in fact exist. Rather, there exist (as Leridon pointed out more than twenty years ago) natural fertility systems, i.e. a relatively wide range of natural situations in which there are reproductive behaviours. At the present time the variation in the number of children is three times greater among populations where a natural fertility system exists than among those which practise birth control.[11] Where there is no conscious desire to limit the number of offspring, family size is determined by a group of factors which are the outcome of living conditions, the way in which society functions or a desire to ensure good health for mother and child. Of particular importance among these factors are variations in the age of puberty and menopause, age at marriage, early widowhood and death, and the duration of breastfeeding and sexual abstinence.

There is not necessarily a link between birth control and access to modern contraceptive methods or even modernization of lifestyles. As the number of case studies has increased, experts have begun to question the generalization of the relationship between industrialization – the symbol of modernity – and fertility transition, i.e. the replacement of a natural fertility system by a situation in which fertility is regulated by contraceptive methods. The decline in fertility in Europe was recorded in some urban environments (Rouen, Geneva, Zurich) as long ago as the end of the seventeenth century. Demographic transition in Europe has more to do with social change than with changes that supposedly released individuals from society's constraints.[12]

To understand family patterns, we must place them within the framework of society's main values, which govern the place occupied by the child. The child is a dimension of the community, the family, the couple and the choices made in order to ensure temporal continuity, as well as a dimension of the life pattern of women and men. Depending on the sociocultural, economic and historical situation, the child represents therefore cheap labour, a guarantee of security in old age or an economic burden. A child's success can be the expression of what the parents were unable to achieve, in which case investment in his or her education is a means of acquiring social status. In present-day Western societies the child continues to fulfil an important function for the mother, the father and the couple, but he or she is competing with other scenarios and is increasingly becoming one possibility among others.

Medicalized Contraception

Although birth control pills and intrauterine devices – not to mention injections and subcutaneous implants – were unknown, the women of earlier generations had on average only three children. Demographic transition in Europe occurred without modern contraceptive means, a good illustration of the fact that these are not essential for changing reproductive behaviour. Modern methods, however, have had a profound impact on fertility: not only have they reduced the number of children more significantly, but also they have in particular reduced the margin of uncertainty inherent in any reproductive behaviour. Individuals and couples adapted to the uncertainty of the relatively effective traditional methods and even turned it to their own advantage. The introduction of modern methods made reproductive patterns, which were essentially imprecise, fluctuating and ambiguous as far as both men and women were concerned, rigid and scarcely capable of change.

The current differences between contraception in the industrialized countries and the countries of the South are striking. A large number of people in the industrialized countries use contraception (between 45 and 80 per cent), but only 45 per cent of them use medicalized contraception. In the countries of the South, contraception use varies enormously (between 0 and 80 per cent), but 84 to 95 per cent of people who use contraception have recourse to medicalized methods. In point of fact, the contraceptive revolution in the countries of the South has a different significance and its course is very different from the course it took in the industrialized nations. In the latter it was part of the overall changes in society, and although individuals were themselves a factor in those changes, they were able to retain some room for manoeuvre regarding available techniques. The concept of family planning is an integral part of individuals' and couples' behaviour, and the diversity of this behaviour is reflected in the wide range of contraceptive methods used. In the countries of the South, on the other hand, modern contraceptive techniques are foreign imports which often clash with local cultural identities[13] and processes of social change. For most people in those countries, a reduction in family size is largely bound up with external influences and access to modern contraceptive methods.

Going beyond North–South differences in women's fertility regulation facilities, one needs to look at their different capabilities as far as mastering contraceptive techniques is concerned, and more broadly at their health and therefore their life patterns. The Programme of Action's recommendations about women and reproduction reveal the need for a radical change of approach, not merely in the way family planning programmes are viewed, but particularly in their integration into a larger set of priorities perceived by women regarding basic health, material and emotional security, and rights.

The practical implementation of the Programme's recommendations requires a closer examination of the role of family planning in meeting women's priority needs, and greater consideration of the activities of the governmental and non-governmental international organizations, which promote contraceptive methods in the countries of the South.

Examining a number of implementation guidelines in the Programme of Action or deriving directly from it helps to identify an initial inconsistency between the spirit of the document and the absolute priority accorded to family planning as regards the funds to be mobilized. The integrated approach desired, whereby family planning is justified as a dimension of women's health, makes the very quality of family planning programmes dependent on the creation of services that first of all provide vital general care. That the Programme's implementation is intended to be confined to contraception, with other fora being left to set up the basic health services, is particularly regrettable. This is because the countries to which reproductive health programmes are most relevant are those where these services are the most inadequate and where women suffer from health problems which make the use of most modern contraceptive methods more difficult.

Table 2.3 *Funds Needed to Implement the Programme of Action (US$millions)*

	Year 2000	Year 2015
Family planning	10.2	13.8
Reproductive health	5.0	6.1
Sexually transmitted diseases	1.3	1.5
Research and analysis	0.5	0.3
Total	17.0	21.7

Moreover, family planning programmes favour highly medicalized contraception – the technical approach inconsistent with the importance accorded to the self-reliance and responsibility of women and men. Since trust is placed in the effectiveness of medicalized contraceptive methods, the aim is undoubtedly to eliminate the failures of poorly managed contraception and thus to solve the problem of pregnancy terminations and their consequences. However, reducing abortion to a failure of contraception, contraception to a technical matter and women to passive patients amounts to treating the symptoms, while forgetting that long-term results cannot be achieved unless the individual is enabled to deal with the causes. Although contraception is an integral dimension of women's health, both of them are components of the broader objectives of family planning and lifelong well-being, i.e. controlling one's life pattern.

The challenge is therefore not only to provide high-quality contraception which is a firmly established part of concern for women's health, but also to give women the means of constructing a genuine life pattern within the space which belongs to them in the community and which they share in the first place with husband and family. Every effort should be made, therefore, to prevent the medicalization of these new approaches from removing women from their context and helping to making them assume by themselves the responsibility for choices. Similarly, efforts should be made to prevent medicalization from subjecting medical consumption to new pressures and thus creating new inequalities between North and South, and between rich and poor. Regarding family planning as a means of exercising free choice, as the Cairo document does, implies that it cannot be in itself the purpose of action and therefore is not a sectoral programme. Rather, it is a dimension of health, inseparable from other problems such as sexually transmitted diseases and AIDS. It is also an integral part of education and the functioning of society, relationships between men and women, and between the rich and the poor, and the various forms of violence these cause.

Freedom of Choice

The second issue suggested by the Programme of Action is the importance of the concept of freedom of choice, since the concepts of individual rights and choices serve nowadays to justify fertility-related action. At least two aspects of the issue require closer analysis. First, a number of countries have reduced their fertility rate considerably by restricting the number of children allowed per couple. Would they have achieved the same result by respecting individual freedom of choice? If not, what would have been the individual and social cost of high population growth extending over several decades? Second, what meaning is to be attached in the West to freedom of choice, bearing in mind that Western societies also restrict the number of children, although they do so by other means, notably the system of values? In that connection, Alfred Perrenoud draws attention to individuals' interiorization of social norms, which operates in such a manner that individuals genuinely view as their own choice what is in reality merely a change in the socially determined family norm.

Individual Freedom of Action is an Illusion
Alfred Perrenoud

The theory of demographic transition is based on the idea that a decrease in child mortality is a precondition for fertility reduction. This presupposes that individuals behave rationally. The weight of subjective factors must become decisive in fertility behaviour so that, freed from social constraints, couples can freely choose to invest or not to invest in their children. As child survival probability increases, this economic and emotional investment becomes greater and generates a desire to limit the number of offspring. This hypothesis, commonly accepted as explaining the decline in fertility in European countries, is at odds with what we know today of the population regulation processes in traditional societies.

First of all, we must expose the idea that large families were seen as a blessing because they provided useful manpower and were an insurance against the uncertainties of life and the risks associated with old age. The belief that past societies, through more or less binding rules, required women to give birth to the maximum number of children does not correspond to reality. There is no society that has not, in one way or another, tended to guide fertility so as to limit its growth while ensuring its own continued existence. In Western society, parents did indeed want to have enough children to help them, but the problem for families was not to have too many children so as to avoid dispersing inheritances.

The rational behaviour ascribed by the theory of demographic transition to those involved is not borne out by the facts. One of the important achievements of a major Princeton University survey to determine the prerequisites for reproductive behaviour change was its demonstration that none of the factors customarily associated with a decrease in fertility – economic development, mortality, child-related costs, women's education and their economic activity, or the dissemination of contraceptive knowledge – appears to be decisive or particularly significant. The great merit of that survey is that it rehabilitated sociocultural explanations, moved the analysis from the individual to the society level and led to norms being considered not as the outcome of a sum of individual actions (which would be explained in terms of the actors' motivation) but as the product of a particular social group, subject to a social logic that is imposed through the values and norms current in society as a whole.

We now know that the decline in fertility in European countries occurred almost simultaneously in profoundly dissimilar economic, social and cultural situations, and therefore that it was part of the same set of dynamics. However, since we are prisoners of causality, we are apt to explain each structural change in terms of a cause external to the particular structure. In point of fact, however, the change exists in the structure itself and in the direction taken by the particular form of social life.

Every society is aware of its physical and economic limits and develops its own population regulation system, based upon a body of standards and practices controlled at all levels of social life – from the individual to the state. These are rules, imposed by the social system, no less binding in modern, 'emancipated' society than in so-called traditional societies. The increasing standardization of fertility behaviours runs counter to the idea of individualization associated with progress. The rise of individualism does not explain the decline in fertility. This is because modernization has not freed individuals from society's constraints, whether family, religious, political or economic; it has merely replaced the old standards and codes of behaviour with new ones. These are the outcome of a slow transformation of social relationships, sustained by an ideology, by values and by a social model which carries within itself the seeds of a genuine family-based economic policy. This model, in which demographic transition is rooted, is the capitalist economy, the product of bourgeois society.

If it is accepted that demographic transition consists in extending a bourgeois standard to the whole of society, we must ask ourselves about the process whereby this new social balance has been achieved. Protestant ethics[14] has probably provided suitable ideological ground. Indeed, Protestant theology helped bring about a certain degree of rational thinking with regard to the family and the economy. Protestant morality contains the seeds of a genuine marriage structure, insofar as it introduces into the family pattern a sense of providence and responsibility, i.e. planning. Calvin believed that God's blessing did not consist of reproduction being left up to divine will, but of children properly educated, looked after and reared, and brought into the world by parents aware of their responsibilities. Similarly, Protestant ethics regards the couple and conjugal union as the normal outcome for human beings. Since the genitals are neither more impure nor less sacred than any other part of the body, the sexual act no longer has to be justified by its purpose – it is God's gift. In this way, the Reformation overturned the prevailing system of values: the child is no longer the primary purpose of marriage, but its consequence.

Strengthened by Protestant ethics, bourgeois morality (which is universalistic and imparts feelings of guilt) introduced a new social order characterized by the general obligation to work, the strict separation of the private and public spheres, and a hierarchy of values based on the primacy of economic success. The spiritual structure resulting from the interiorization of bourgeois standards produced various social phenomena. The most important of these, from the point of view of changes in reproductive behaviour, are: desocialization and withdrawal into the family, the latter increasing the child's dependence on its parents and the distance between the adult and the child; and the emphasis on the value of work as a means of achieving redemption, and on the value of success, moderation and self-restraint – i.e. a rationalization of performance. The spirit and essence of this system of values were at variance with unregulated reproduction. The body – the organ of pleasure – was transformed into an organ of performance, since bourgeois sexuality accepted only the bare minimum, namely that which is useful –in this case reproduction. As far as the family was concerned, this self-control and prudence led to action to combat the waste inherent in early mortality, and then to women's return to the home in their maternal functions – the only accepted ones because they were regarded as the only useful ones. Lastly, self-control and prudence made people thrifty about the number of children brought into the world. The Industrial Revolution removed women from reproductive functions; they entered the new industrial order through poverty, with the result that they were enslaved by their status not as women but as workers. These changes occurred while the structure of women's life cycles was undergoing profound changes due to the fact that people were living longer and marrying later, and an increasing number were not marrying at all.

As far as the engines of change are concerned, while the contraceptive revolution at the end of the nineteenth century and the present-day one differ in terms of methods and scale, there has been no fundamental change. The context in which individuals make their choice is still the product of an ideology. Each society sets a standard for fertility and reproduction that is bound up with social relationships and with its image of itself. As Chantal Blayo says, 'the fact that individuals adhere to system-imposed rules does not mean that they are not rules. Perhaps the medicalization of contraception is therefore merely an official means of compelling women to have the number of children that society expects of them'.

The same applies to the liberalization of morals, which may be interpreted in the light of the economic requirements of a consumer society that has resurrected desire and pleasure as consumer items. In such a system of civilization, in which hedonism and personal enjoyment are set up as models justified by the notions of individual freedom and development, it is difficult to see where children fit in. The time for consumption, the time when everything is possible, is adolescence. Unlike childhood, which is forward-looking and future-oriented, it is unstable and short-lived. We may well wonder what the future holds in store for a society that promotes everything that is ephemeral, and constantly strives to absolve individuals of all responsibility.

The value system created by post-industrial society – in which consumerism and the quest for instant well-being and instant everything take precedence over investment – is in opposition to the family and the child. The child competes with the economy and has become a consumer product to which one is entitled because it is in the marketplace. This accounts for the growing impatience of women who, believing they are sterile, demand the right to avail themselves of reproduction technology and all its aberrations.

Whether we like it or not, the combination of biogenetic progress, predictive medicine, medically assisted reproduction technology and the social demand for children at any price, at any age, free from abnormalities and hereditary diseases, and of a specific sex, is leading us towards a society based on eugenics. Imprisoned in a system of values that requires individuals to perform in certain ways, will we be able to avoid the worst, i.e. the search for the best? Lacking knowledge, transcendent wisdom or universal harmony to which we can refer to answer that question, we shall need to determine for whom and on what grounds the best will be chosen. Must we therefore leave it to science to guide us in making that determination and to set the boundaries of good and evil? In today's world that question is ever present.

Freedom of choice, as understood in the Cairo document, assumes that the individual as *Homo oeconomicus* is both autonomous and rational. But isn't the concept of autonomy itself dependent on different conceptions of the world, each with its own requirements and own promises, as indicated by the differences in approach between Buddhism and Catholicism?

Other Conceptions of the World: Buddhism and Catholicism

The definition of autonomy varies from culture to culture. In Buddhism, it consists in freeing oneself from suffering, not from situation-dependent sufferings constituted by physical pain, annoyances and vexations, but a deep, permanent suffering that is part of the human condition and cannot be eradicated except by means of deprogramming techniques. According to Buddha's teaching, being autonomous means 'being within oneself as on an island' and overcoming a sense of affliction. This sense derives from ignorance, which is a false knowledge that, unbeknown to us, sets itself up as true; from the belief in our own existence that causes us to say 'I am' and identify ourselves with this 'I'; from passion, whether attraction or aversion; and from the unreasoning desire for life.

Buddhism holds that individualism, with its succession of demands, is a sickness and that individual freedom of choice is meaningless. Autonomy is achieved only after a person has matured during countless different lives. While he or she awaits the extinction of conditioned life and the suffering inherent in it, the Buddhist's cardinal virtue is patience, a characteristic which embodies the originality of the Indian sensitivity to suffering. The patience of Buddhists, explains Guy Bugault,[15] represents acceptance of the fundamental law of existence – change and impermanence – and compassion for all creatures, which makes the suffering person say: 'my suffering is but a drop of water in the ocean of universal suffering'. The doctrine underpinning this is that of *karma*, according to which our present situation is the result of our experience and actions in previous lives. However this belief is viewed, its virtue is that it both explains and soothes: it makes inequalities of birth and rank easier to understand, since they are felt less as injustices. And it opens the way to hope: it is my lot today, but things may be otherwise tomorrow if I take the necessary action. 'The Indian soul has no notion of tragedy because tragedy cannot exist unless time stops; in India, nothing is ever irrevocable, even unhappy things come to an end.'[16]

Catholicism has a totally different view of autonomy, one that is under-pinned by its doctrine and by the diversity of believers' individual viewpoints. In the course of lengthy family pastoral work with couples in Belgium during the 1960s and 1970s, Father Pierre de Locht sought the means of entrenching autonomy in the Christian faith, i.e. ensuring that autonomy strengthened it while at the same time freeing humankind. According to Father de Locht, autonomy is that which compels human beings to accept their destiny, to take greater responsibility for it, to begin – painfully and pleasurably – the difficult task of building a harmonious world. Autonomy in no way signifies egocen-trism, individual or collective, set up as standards. It implies the requirement to increasingly internalize the standards by which one acts. In his view,[17] being wholly responsible and being answerable for the history of mankind and universal solidarity, while increasing the commitment to our personal and collective future, do not destroy religious faith in any way. But religious faith is no longer necessarily the distress call of blind humanity: it can become, in freedom and maturity, the welcome accorded to transcendence, to a love that is offered over and above any need or compulsion. Faith is within the realm of meaning, a complement of meaning. It does not give a satisfactory answer to the painful questions that arise from encounters with evil, the suffering of innocent people and death. However, by not closing our world in on itself, faith broadens the issue, acknowledging a vast open space that looks not onto the void but onto life.

Starting from a wholly different reasoning, Paul Valadier concurs with Father de Locht when he says that 'the Church should help reason to assert itself and to recover the courage in its power... If faith has a meaning, it lies in its helping mankind to arise and to walk, and in its summoning reason to its own court to help it rediscover the meaning of...reason... Faith lives on the certainty that even in the worst predicaments, mankind can always find a way out'.[18]

Women's Work Outside the Home and the Well-being of Children

The Programme of Action calls for a closer analysis of the relationships between number of children, women's employment and family well-being. Research by Alaka Basu in India and Frédéric de Coninck in France demonstrates that although paid employment opens up new possibilities for women's self-fulfilment, the sociocultural context in which women decide whether to work outside the home radically alters the consequences of their decision, both for themselves and for the well-being of their children.

The Case of India

As a result of economic modernization currently under way, a number of poor women are now able to work outside the home. Alaka Basu[19] has shown that being a child in an Indian family that is both poor and 'modern' is the worst of all possible worlds. Her study of the relationships between family size and children's well-being revealed that the number of children was relevant only in relation to a particular context and that it might have a number of very different consequences for family well-being. In her view, the main point is that the cost of modernity in terms of individual well-being is not revealed by conventional indicators of economic progress (urbanization and GDP growth).

Nowadays, large population groups are increasingly required to make choices in a situation which may be described as modernization in poverty. In urban areas, families have two choices: to provide their children with education or to take advantage of the income-earning opportunities available to them, particularly women and children (for whom opportunities exist in the service industries). Unfortunately, however, these two choices are incompatible for poor families. Because of their scanty resources, the only solution is to choose from among their children those who will have to pay the price of this incompatibility, and it will be the girls more often than the boys who are chosen. It also happens sometimes that although some boys in a family go to school, their brothers remain illiterate.

Working women reap some benefits: access to material resources (income) and non-material resources (information). And of course they gain in terms of independence. On the other hand, working is not compatible with their children's well-being, particularly since family and community mutual assistance networks are underdeveloped or non-existent in urban areas. Even where they exist, they do not make up for the mother's absence.

The outcome for the child is higher infant mortality and/or a more stringent choice between those who will go to school and those who will stay at home to do household work. Those poor families in which the mother works have higher infant mortality than those families with the same amount of income in which the mother does not work. In policy terms, Alaka Basu concludes that women's work and child care have to be separated. This means, among other things, improving child-care centres and modifying women's working conditions to enable them to combine these two functions. But how can that be done in an under-industrialized or non-industrialized economy in which women do the bulk of their work in an informal sector that is itself increasingly precarious?

The Case of France

In a completely different context – France from the 1960s to the 1990s – Frédéric de Coninck and Francis Godard[20] have attempted to identify the main features of the radical changes in women's employment and family structures. Their analysis puts into perspective the relationships between women's increased activity outside the home, their increasing independence, choosing the time of the first child's birth and the conditions under which a couple's life is negotiated.

For many women, employment opens up a new range of possibilities: to live as a married couple or to remain single; to have a job before beginning married life or not to have one; to have a child or not to have one; to have a child soon after starting married life or to postpone doing so. The conflict between working life and family life gives rise to another alternative, one closely bound up with the advancement of women's careers: that is whether to stay married or to get divorced. A woman's educational qualifications guide her initial choices and the way she plans her life. They give her time; she does not have to start her working life too soon; and she can postpone the birth of her first child. Later, as time passes, her working life becomes more important and, after her first child has been born, her overall career prospects guide her choices.

Because of the amount of time that women devote to reproduction and to child-rearing, the use of their time is an important factor in the Cairo Programme of Action. Whereas reproduction once took up two-fifths of women's married life, the figure in industrialized nations[21] is now an average of one-thirtieth. Birth control is therefore regarded as a way for women in other regions of the world to considerably reduce their workload. The Programme of Action stresses not only the relationship between a decline in the number of births and better use of women's time, but also planning the appropriate time for pregnancy. This enables women to cope better with pregnancy – that is, without its endangering their health or competing with their other aspirations. To that end, managing reproduction is recognized as being inseparable from the overall management of women's time, tasks and many roles.

The Diverse Types of Family

The diversity of national and individual situations requires guidelines that are more sensitive to the complexity of current changes and, in particular, are not based on only one model. Taking the case of the African family, Thérèse Locoh emphasizes the many different facets of changes that are increasingly departing from recognized models and the types of family expected as a result of modernization and development.

African Family Types
Thérèse Locoh

According to Jean-Pierre Olivier de Sardan, 'there has been a great tendency throughout the history of the social sciences to regard all non-Western societies as a group with specific features, whereas in some ways all such societies have little in common other than the fact that they are not Western society'.[22]

The African family comprises several mutually inclusive concepts: the biological family, whose members may or may not live together; the domestic unit, representing a production entity which has shared accommodation; and the family institutions corresponding to the ideology regulating family lifestyles, i.e. gender-based roles, norms governing the marriage contract, norms governing reproduction and access to property, and residential rules. The nuclearization of the African family, which had been expected as a sign of modernization and social change, does not seem to be happening. On the contrary, it is the poorest households that live as nuclear families – not the most modern ones. Respect for the elderly and their authority over young people are a key element in family institutions. Consequently men, and women even more so, will become independent at a very late stage. Family solidarity extends beyond the domestic unit; and in urban areas, where great demands are made of it, it is beginning to be stretched to its limits. The positive side to this compulsory solidarity is that it enables a needy person to be helped; but its downside is that it gives preference to the survival and expansion of extended family groups rather than to individual aspirations. As a result, greater store is set by family solidarity than by solidarity between husband and wife. Marriages based on strong emotional ties between spouses are therefore still in the minority.

Since most of them have suffered large-scale demographic catastrophes – the slave trade, forced labour, shortages, epidemics, excess mortality of crisis proportions – African societies have devised survival strategies over the generations. While investment in human labour remains the basic means of increasing output, reproduction continues to be the mainspring of the family system and institutions develop standards to safeguard it. These include early marriage of women, remarriage of widows, polygamy, child care within the extended family, and holding in high esteem adults who have a high fertility rate. Moreover, since progress in reducing infant mortality is still uncertain, at least as regards a large part of the population, it is deemed necessary to maintain high fertility so as to be prepared for the worst. Consequently, marriage customs foster high fertility. Marriage is first and foremost an alliance between two families. For the newlyweds it is followed by integration into a broader residential group which more often than not, in the countryside, is a production unit. Relations between spouses are characterized by a strict division of rights and duties, which is reinforced by the continuing close solidarity with each spouse's family. Conjugal relations are frequently marred by mistrust, particularly because of polygamy. Children are the only means that women have of making their status permanent. Moreover, the movement of children within the extended family weakens the cause-and-effect relationship between childbearing and the cost of a child's maintenance and education. Even though the objective conditions for generations' survival have changed, societies' production and reproduction values continue to influence behaviour. Societies need time to alter their standards in accordance with new demographic situations – the time it takes for these new situations to be perceived and for a change in behaviour to be deemed necessary.

Very different situations are masked by the stereotypical image of the African continent uniformly maintaining high fertility levels (five to seven children per woman, i.e. a 3 per cent annual growth and the doubling of the population within 23 years). Profound changes are under way. Fertility has declined in half of the 17 countries for which we have recent data. In at least three countries – Kenya, Zimbabwe and Botswana – the trend is well established and is also manifest, nearly everywhere, in urban areas. In a number of countries, people are becoming aware that 'children no longer die as they used to'. There are other changes but for the time being they are mutually exclusive in terms of fertility: modern methods of contraception are making headway in urban areas, but at the same time the use of traditional means of spacing births, including postnatal sexual abstinence and breastfeeding, is decreasing. There is a new demand for contraception, particularly among unmarried adults and adolescents, who have so far been more or less excluded from contraceptive programmes. Similarly, men's involvement in these programmes is inadequate.

The economic crisis affects fertility and the family in many different ways. The burden on adults, particularly women, is growing while insignificant state initiatives to defray social expenditure are called into question or simply abandoned. The number of orphans is growing because of AIDS. Unemployment compels women to make greater efforts to feed their families. The lack of economic prospects reduces young people's access to independent earnings outside family control. The crisis is causing roles to be redefined. It is too early to say whether women and young people – the traditional dependants of household heads – will achieve greater independence as a result of this redefinition or will once again lose out in the changes under way. New family codes are emerging, but they have very little influence on real life.

The Unpopularity of Marriage Continues

With all due respect to the upholders of tradition, marriage is no longer popular. In 1993, a total of 255,200 marriages were celebrated in France, 6 per cent fewer than the previous year. This figure, the century's lowest peace-time one, stabilized in 1994 at about 254,000 ... although people of marriageable age, especially those in the 20–30 age bracket, belong to generations in which there are many children... There was a slight increase in the number of marriages between 1988 and 1990, but it did not continue owing to the economic crisis, and also to unemployment, which makes it difficult for young couples to set up home... Nowadays, one 35- year-old woman in five is unmarried, and 15 per cent of women aged 40 are not married and have not been married. Only 9 per cent of women born in 1943 were in that situation at the same age... It is expected that a growing number of women will remain unmarried for the rest of their lives.

Le Monde, *March 1995, Paris*

Polygamy is unchanged and, contrary to expectation, nuclear families are still not playing a part in improving the status of women. It seems that owing to work-related migration and various forms of mobility linked to men's economic activities, the situation is moving towards one of multipolar households with co-spouses living in different areas – in other words, a more modern form of polygamy. Moreover, the number of unmarried couples living together is increasing because those concerned do not have the money needed to pay marriage indemnities. The proportion of households headed by women is also increasing. This is sometimes indicative of women's greater independence but more often means that a woman has been deserted by a husband no longer able to fulfil his responsibilities as head of the family.

Rather than moving towards a dominant model, African families are moving towards increasing diversification, which is the result of a compromise between traditional norms, imported new models and values, and constraints imposed by the deteriorating economic situation. Without doubt, the beginnings of a decline in fertility which are now observable will bring about further changes in family dynamics.

Wives and Concubines

In the last fifteen or so years, some hundreds of thousands of Hong Kong business-men and clerical staff have gone to the People's Republic of China to try their luck... Since there are considerable living standard differences between China, Hong Kong and Taiwan, for the most part [they] have gone on their own. Far away from their wives for long periods, they have started to have extramarital relations and have ended up leading double lives, with women and illegitimate children in China... The social services and the Association of Hong Kong Women are receiv-ing a growing number of requests for help from wives abandoned by husbands working in China... According to a number of surveys, seven Taiwanese business-men out of ten working in China are committing adultery... In a matter of this sort, one can talk ad infinitum about human nature and morality. The real prob-lem, however, is its future cost in social terms... The number of illegitimate children in China will run into hundreds of thousands. It will hardly be possible to refuse them the right to be reunited with their fathers for the purpose of secur-ing recognition and their share of any inheritance... To curb this trend, there has to be cooperation between the three countries to make it easier for businessmen to go to China with their families. If they are accompanied, one of the main reasons for infidelity will no longer exist.

Yazhou Zhoukan, February 1995, Hong Kong

Chapter 3
Population and Development

Development, the last word in the title of the Cairo Conference, was supposed to be the cornerstone of that gathering. This was to be achieved through renewed discussion of the relationships between demographic change and development factors within the framework of the concept of sustainable development, adopted by the international community in Rio. In reality, however, development remained the poor relation, and the few development-related measures in the Programme of Action are those for harmonizing population and development trends. They are summarized below.

Population and Development: Programme of Action

Rights and Principles

The right to development is a universal and inalienable right and an integral part of fundamental human rights. It must be fulfilled so as to equitably meet the population, development and environment needs of present and future generations. While development facilitates the enjoyment of all human rights, the lack of development may not be invoked to justify the abridgment of internationally recognized human rights.

Individuals have the right to a healthy and productive life in harmony with nature, and to an adequate standard of living for themselves and their families, including food, clothing, housing and drinking water. Human beings are at the centre of concerns for sustainable development, and they are the most important and valuable resource of any nation. Demographic goals and policies form part of cultural, economic and social development, and are directed principally at improving the quality of life of all people. Even the difference of a single decade in the transition to stabilization levels of fertility can have a considerable positive impact on quality of life.

All countries should recognize their common but differentiated responsibilities. Sustainable development requires that the interrelationships between population, resources, the environment and development should be fully recognized, properly managed and brought into harmonious, dynamic balance.

Objective

Population concerns must be fully integrated into development strategies, planning, decision-making and resource allocation at all levels and in all regions, with the goal of meeting the needs, and improving the quality of life, of present and future generations.

Economic Measures

Sustained economic growth within the framework of sustainable development is essential to eradicate poverty. Population growth puts strains on weak economies because of the investment necessary for meeting the needs of a growing population: education, sanitation, water, housing, food and productive jobs.

The persistence of poverty and social and gender inequities impacts negatively on population trends. Poverty is often accompanied by unemployment, illiteracy, low status of women, exposure to environmental risks, limited access to social and health services, inappropriate spatial distribution of population, inequitable distribution of natural resources and environmental degradation. To slow down population growth, governments must reduce poverty.

Sustainable development should be supported by appropriate macroeconomic policies, good governance, effective national policies and efficient national institutions. Unsustainable patterns of consumption and production contribute to environmental degradation. The developed countries should take the lead in achieving sustainable consumption patterns and efficient waste management programmes through economic, legislative and administrative measures consistent with sustainable development criteria.

The developed countries acknowledge the responsibility that they bear in the international pursuit of sustainable development, and should improve their efforts to promote sustained economic growth and narrow imbalances affecting the developing countries.

Areas of Action

There are four priorities in combating poverty and meeting the needs of a growing world population: provision of food security through the strengthening of food and agriculture programmes and policies; creation of jobs in industry, agriculture and services; decentralization of production and decision-making structures; and investment in human resources.

Development implies long-term sustainability in production and consumption relating to all economic activities, including agriculture. Measures should be taken to strengthen food, nutrition and agricultural policies and programmes, establish fair trade relations and achieve food security.

Education enables individuals to exercise their fundamental rights and meet their needs through full participation in society. Education and vocational training are essential because they determine individual access to employment opportunities and health, and provide an alternative to early marriages, particularly for young girls. Governments, the private sector and non-governmental organizations should therefore invest in human resources, and promote and evaluate the education and skill development of women and young girls.

Jobs must be created, particularly for disadvantaged and vulnerable populations. In formulating their employment policies, countries must bear in mind the need to enable men and women to combine work and family responsibilities. In addition, they should ensure women's access to the labour market so that they can have their own income, which is a prerequisite for economic self-reliance.

Spatial Distribution of Population and Economic Activities

The administrative system and production structures should be decentralized so as to enable municipal, local and regional bodies to play a leading role in development. To that end, governments should give increased financial responsibilities to regional and municipal bodies.

To cope with migration from rural areas, countries are called upon to adopt a development strategy designed to stabilize urbanization and develop small or medium-sized urban centres, thereby enabling the creation of jobs in rural areas and the better distribution of production and population. That involves the setting up of efficient transport systems, the training of young people in non-agricultural trades and a labour-intensive economic strategy. To encourage decentralized economic development, governments should adopt a policy encouraging the relocation of industries and businesses to rural areas, particularly through the provision of incentives to those employers who will create non-agricultural rural jobs.

With regard to urban areas, governments should restructure urban management bodies in order to ensure better soil, air, water and waste management, as well as sound use and protection of fragile ecosystems.

Environment

The population explosion, population distribution and migration may put pressure on the environment, particularly in vulnerable ecosystems. A healthy environment is necessary if the basic needs of growing populations are to be met. The lands of indigenous people must be protected from environmentally unsound activities. Generally speaking, countries should increase environmental protection education.

Countries must achieve the population and environment objectives of Agenda 21 (which was agreed at the Rio Conference) – namely, to utilize demographic data to promote sustainable resource management; to implement policies which address the ecological implications of population growth; and to undertake research into the linkages among population trends, consumption, production, natural resources and health.

The Programme of Action introduces three elements: the objective of making the economic system 'sustainable'; the need to stimulate economic growth in order to combat poverty; and the right to development. They are new, however, in a terminological rather than a conceptual sense, since the Programme merely borrowed the ideas of other conferences held in the 1990s. For example, it took the concept of sustainable development from the Rio environment conference and the concept of the right to development from the Vienna human rights conference. Like other conferences, it gives priority to action to combat poverty and protect the poorest groups of people.

The Framework of Sustainability

The Bucharest Conference recommended a 'form of development promoting the balanced and efficient consumption of resources'. The Cairo Programme of Action takes up the same theme, updating the terminology and adapting its framework to that of 'sustainability'. Socioeconomic development is replaced by 'sustainable development', with a considerable number of interdependent factors invoked: environmental degradation, population growth, poverty, health, human rights, education, status of women, equitable international trade relations, human resources, social justice, decentralization, and so forth. Macro and micro factors from the economic, political, ecological and sociocultural fields are freely mixed in, without any explanation of the relevance of the linkages or how the Programme of Action will actually be able to channel their impacts to the desired end.

Sustained Economic Growth to Combat Poverty

For the first time ever, a population action document explicitly recommended that economic growth be stimulated. It had not previously been stated that the need for growth applied to development, probably because in the 1970s and 1980s this was so obvious that there seemed perhaps no point in spelling it out. The situation is different today, however. For some people, the concept of sustainable development implies an end to growth measured solely in terms of material output, and the use of other criteria to reveal the different individually and socially created forms of wealth – intellectual, emotional, artistic, biological and so on.

The objective of economic growth goes hand in hand with action to combat poverty, the result being that both are seen as the two dimensions of one and the same strategy. The eradication of poverty is put forward as a condition, if not the most important one, for stabilizing the world population. Pursuing that line, the Programme therefore focuses on vulnerable groups and/or the most disadvantaged ones: women, indigenous peoples, the elderly,

---

In the news

Growth has Created Imbalances

The National Bank reports that the Thai Gross National Product has reached 8.5 per cent growth. The average per capita income of Thais has reached 60,000 baht [approximately US$ 2353], raising Thailand from the status of a developing country to an industrialised nation...

[C]apital distribution in Thailand fails to alleviate stress faced by people in rural areas. Development will take place, no doubt, but who will benefit and who will be left out?...

We are considered a modern society, but in many ways we are still not developed. Why is the Government so often unable to uplift the majority of people, the poor who live far from Bangkok? It is because the Thai economy is dominated by large corporations and monopolies run by a few top families, their relatives and friends...

The disparities among economic interest groups can be seen starkly in the plight of our hilltribe people who often find their forest habitat encroached on by powerful companies and individuals, exploiting and gobbling up 'protected' land for their own enrichment...

We must beware of economic policies that blunt the effects of equal opportunity and development for the majority of the population. Although there may be those privileged few holding a big piece of the cake, will they enjoy eating it with the poor crowding the streets and clamouring at their gates? It is only the powerful elite, in cooperation with planners and administrators, who gain from this kind of progress.

Prayat Punong-ong, The Bangkok Post, *February 1995, Bangkok*

---

migrants, families, very young girls, children, the unemployed and people with disabilities. Moreover, it stresses that sustained economic growth must be achieved within the framework of sustainable development.

The Right to Development

The right to development is presented as an essential factor in achieving equity among nations. The Programme does not make clear, however, whether this right belongs to individuals, peoples, states or nations. Neither does it explain the possible mechanisms for guaranteeing its implementation or the linkages between it and the various aspects of population. Nevertheless, it has to be said in defence of the Cairo negotiators that such a task would have been impossible, because since its appearance on the international scene[1] the 'right to development' has been devoid of substance. Despite the undoubted efforts of many committees and groups of experts requested to give it a meaning, its nature, and even more so its specific implications, remain undefined.

The debate on the interrelationships between population and development was only superficial and therefore made little impression on the general direction taken by the Programme of Action. The presence of the development issue is due to the juxtaposition of a number of standard formulations rather than to the elaboration of a particular line of thought. The superficial treatment of this issue is made all the more obvious by the in-depth and pragmatic discussion of fertility. Whereas the reproductive health recommendations go as far as such technical matters as the 'provision of micronutrient supplementation and tetanus toxoid' to pregnant women, the development recommendations are restricted to stating that 'the achievement of sustainable development and poverty eradication should be supported by macroeconomic policies designed to provide an appropriate international economic environment'. The Programme has no particular position regarding the causes of the problems, which remain ill defined; and the goals pursued and the modes of action lack consistency. Lastly, the recommendations contain few specific guidelines for moving from the general to the specific, and from theory to practice.

The World Plan of Action on Population, adopted in Bucharest in 1974, was based on the following assessment:

> 'The consideration of population problems cannot be reduced to the analysis of population trends only ... the present situation of the developing countries originates in the unequal processes of socio-economic development which have divided peoples since the beginning of the modern era. This inequity still exists and is intensified by lack of equity in international economic relations with consequent disparity in levels of living.'

For its part, the Cairo Programme of Action merely juxtaposes *de facto* situations in such a way as to suggest many different causes, none of which is ever spelt out:

> 'the developing countries are still facing serious economic difficulties and an unfavourable international economic environment, and the number of people living in absolute poverty has increased in many countries. Around the world many of the basic resources on which future generations will depend for their survival and well-being are being depleted and environmental degradation is intensifying, driven by unsustainable patterns of production and consumption, unprecedented growth in population, widespread and persistent poverty, and social and economic inequality.'

Despite a certain amount of terminological face-lifting, the measures proposed in the Cairo document are consistent with the approach of the 1970s and 1980s and do not correspond to current realities. Whether in the fields of food security, job creation or urban management, new perspectives are now essential for the elaboration of effective solutions to present and future challenges. At the theoretical level, the debate is based on two implicit axioms, which at the very least deserve to be studied more closely and invoked more discriminatingly since they have never been validated scientifically. The first holds that population growth is a factor in poverty, and the second that it plays a significant role in environmental degradation. Both axioms will be discussed later in this chapter.

There are at least three reasons for the lack of debate and commitment regarding the development issue. First, the preference given to reproduction and women oriented the Conference in a particular direction. Added to that is the relationship which developed among those participating in the preparatory process. Unlike in Bucharest and Mexico City, where the discussions were between economists and planners, in Cairo a substantial number of participants – both within the government delegations and among the non-governmental organizations – were from the health, family planning and women's affairs sectors. In the opinion of Walter Mertens,[2] the importance of the non-governmental organizations played a large part in focusing attention on their areas of concern to the detriment of a broader macroeconomic perspective. This is because those organizations are particularly involved in microsocial activities; they have very little scientific knowledge regarding demography and development economics, and are more interested in advocacy than in problem analysis.

Second, delegations' lack of interest in development reveals a fundamental trend in the present international debate – the trend towards political abdication. If 'what is important in political debate is less what is said than what is actually done [it has to be noted that] politicians are increasingly suggesting that "nothing can be done"'.[3] The political debate on development has continued to decline since the 1970s. In 1974, the UN General Assembly placed on its agenda the question of the New World Economic Order, which was regarded as the requisite framework for any discussion of the sectoral aspects of development, including population. The industrialized nations, however, refused to debate it and, for want of interlocutors, the demands for this New World Economic Order by the countries of the South gradually faded away. Towards the end of the 1970s and the beginning of the 1980s, the Non-Aligned Movement called for a New World Information and Communication Order, but this call also proved unsuccessful.

Nowadays, the political mobilization of states around the main development issues is virtually non-existent. Now that it has no more challenges (apartheid and Palestine – the two main issues of the 1980s – are regarded as closed), the political debate is going nowhere. The development theories propounded in the 1960s, which are now obsolete, have not been replaced by a coherent political vision of the future. From the present ideological desert there emerges only a strong desire for economic growth at any price, a desire shared by governments as dissimilar as those of the Western industrialized nations and the former European people's democracies, and the socialist, communist, military or civilian regimes of the other continents. The Rio consensus on sustainable development has not yet revived the international debate. This is not only because the concept itself is still vague and interpreted in very different ways, but also because it cannot be implemented until the principles of economic and social sustainability have been defined and tested locally. Although many new social and economic practices are currently being tried out, the fact that they have not yet been analysed means that it is too early to draw universally applicable lessons from them. Consequently, the sustainable development debate is likely to remain theoretical for a number of years yet – more a sort of incantation than anything else.

The third reason for the lack of attention to development and, generally speaking, to analysis of the macro dimension of economic and social changes is the direction taken by scientific population research. As will be seen later,[4] the study of population and development, largely by experts from the English-speaking world, has been relatively superficial compared with fertility research. Harriet Presser[5] has demonstrated this fact in an analysis that is as simple as it is revealing. Comparing the topics dealt with by the members of the Population Association of America at congresses, meetings and workshops in the 1960s and 1980s,[6] she notes that these population specialists concentrated on fertility, the family, methodology and migration, development being relegated to the remaining third of the topics considered.

The observations of Paul Demeny confirm this trend. In the US,

'funding for population research by the Federal Government is generous ... total federal support for population research ... in fiscal year 1992 amounted to $284 million. These funds financed over 1100 research projects. Only two among these could be classified as research on the "consequences of population change". Neither of these had anything to do with the impact of rapid population growth on economic development ... together [they] received $175 000, or less than one-tenth of one percent of total federal funding for population research.'[7]

Furthermore, the scientific community is relatively excluded from the preparation of intergovernmental conferences. Generally speaking, and not only in the population field, the role of 'experts' in organizing United Nations conferences has been progressively reduced in favour of a political and technocratic approach. In the case of the Cairo population conference, despite the existence of six expert groups, the scientific contribution to the debate was slight except in the areas of reproduction and women.

The combination of the three factors just described enabled negotiators to content themselves with a relatively loose argument based on two axioms that appeal to commonsense but are scientifically unproved. Since it is easy to slip from a simple idea to an incorrect one, it is worthwhile briefly reconsidering these axioms in the light of considerations that reveal the full complexity of the situations they encompass.

Two Axioms to be Put into Context

The Linkages between Poverty and High Fertility

Statistics reveal higher fertility rates in low GDP regions than in high GDP countries (with exceptions such as the Gulf nations). Various aspects of poverty – low level of education, inferior status of women and high infant mortality – impact negatively on fertility reduction. However, for several years now new data and various observations have indicated a significant decline in fertility coupled with a state of poverty. This phenomenon, identified first in Latin America by Maria Cosio-Zavala and termed by her the 'Malthusianism of poverty', explains the effects of the economic crisis on the poorest families. A drop in the standard of living, unemployment, malnutrition and shortages of all sorts have resulted in an appreciable decline in their fertility.

Does population growth cause poverty? Massimo Livi-Bacci[8] says that those mechanisms operating at the macrosocial level have to be considered separately from those that are meaningful solely at the level of individual behaviour. At the macroeconomic level, the question is closely linked to the relationship between population growth and development, about which no conclusive data or analyses yet exist. At this level, the significant element is not population growth but the impoverishment mechanism associated with social and economic change. Overall, fertility, mortality and family size are greater among the poor, but this should not be mistaken for a causal link. 'In the social sciences, causality is probabilistic and statistical, not logical... A social cause does not explain a risk (i.e. a probability) but occurs as a risk factor (that which modifies probability)... Analysis of causality leads one to doubt the relevance of the very concept of cause and to prefer the concept of a changing system.'[9]

At the individual level, Livi-Bacci draws attention to the interrelationships between those demographic events around which every person's life is structured (family formation, reproduction, migration, mortality) and the risks or otherwise of being poor. These events affect an individual's ability to achieve well-being or, at the very least, to avoid poverty. Marriage, children and migration, for example, are options for minimizing life's risks. At the population level, these options provide the degree of flexibility essential for group survival. 'The greater the flexibility, the more extensive the population's choices for responding to constraints.'[10]

Various models endeavour to explain the underdevelopment of the countries of the South: the modernization theory invokes economic and cultural backwardness; and neo-Marxist and dependence theories refer to imperialism, with development and underdevelopment as the two aspects of the same historical process. In its efforts to combat underdevelopment the Cairo Programme of Action concentrates on combating poverty, which is itself the subject of various theoretical approaches. Bruno Lautier[11] sets out at least three which are current in international organizations today.

The first of these describes poverty pathologically: poverty is a disease to be eradicated by means of special strategies for the poor. At United Nations conferences in recent years countless hours have been devoted to choosing the appropriate verb: is poverty to be *eliminated, reduced, eradicated* or *removed*, or are its effects to be *eased*?

The second approach views poverty as a social and political danger which has to be neutralized by social welfare provision, re-education and punishment. This approach is all the more ambiguous since it is not clear what constitutes the threat: the poor as individuals or poverty as a manifestation of the unravelling of social ties. It is at the core of the dispute between supporters and opponents of family planning in the countries of the South. Opponents argue that birth control advocates do not want to eliminate poverty but to liquidate the poor.

The third approach is particularly common among politically committed non-governmental organizations and churches. Help for the poor is generally based on helping them to organize themselves, the idea of combating poverty subtly becoming the concept of solidarity among the poor themselves.

The development strategy advocated since the 1980s is based on compulsory structural adjustment, with safety nets to cushion its effects on the poorest people. Since the crisis has worsened rather than lessened in many countries, the positive idea of development has been gradually abandoned in favour of action on poverty and provision of emergency humanitarian aid. For that reason, the strategy of the Cairo Programme, like that of other United Nations action plans of the 1990s, is essentially based on so-called at-risk groups. Paul Demeny considers this approach a methodological dead end because if 'Children, adolescents, women, the aged, the disabled, indigenous people[s], rural populations, urban populations, migrants, refugees, displaced persons and slum-dwellers ... are the underserved, who should be their servers?'[12]

┌─ *In the news* ───

Allowances Are Better Than Prison

The unemployment rate in the United States is low. Unfortunately, however, many people are in prison. According to the New York Times *there were 4.2 million out of work in 1993, as against 4.6 million in prison. 'Our prison population is the equivalent of the long-term unemployment in Europe,' says Richard Freeman, a Harvard economist. 'We lock people up, young and not so young, poor and largely uneducated. We feed them, and give them televisions. But the problem remains.'*

Courrier international, *No. 227, 9–15 March 1995, Paris*

Although poverty is certainly less widespread than in the countries of the South, it nevertheless exists in OECD countries, the number of badly-off people having increased considerably. The governments represented in Cairo scarcely mentioned that fact at all, confining themselves to recommendations to the countries of the South. Poverty in the industrialized countries is unrelated to population growth, which on no account is responsible for the growing income disparities between the richest segment of the population and the poorest one. These disparities continued to increase throughout the 1980s in most of the 24 nations of the Western world.

> '*The US is by far the country with the greatest income differences. The range is almost from one to six between the richest 10 per cent and the poorest 10 per cent, compared with proportions of 4.7 per cent in Belgium, 6.5 per cent in Germany and 7.5 per cent in France. The US is different from other countries by reason both of the greater proportion of poor people and of their low level of income compared with the rest of the population. At the end of the 1980s, 18 per cent of Americans were living below the poverty line.*'[13]

┌─ In the news ──┐

The High Price of the US Employment Miracle

'*Differences in income are greater here than in any other industrialized country*', says Robert Reich, Bill Clinton's Secretary of Labor. '*We cannot have a stable and prosperous society if this trend continues.*' Despite the economic upturn, average per household income decreased in 1993, and more than a million people fell below the poverty line. A total of 15.1 per cent of the population is deemed to be living in poverty... Social inequality has social costs — an increase in health care expenditure, the number of homeless and the crime rate. These have to be borne by the economy as a whole, and they hinder growth.

Nikolaus Piper, Die Zeit, *March 1995, Hamburg*

└──┘

Population Growth and Environmental Degradation

The upside to environmental degradation is that it has made us aware that the world is finite and that nature's ability to resist the harm done to it by humankind is not unlimited. Humankind, says Hubert Greppin,[14] behaved in the past like a growing bacterium that sought to take up all available space and use everything in it. Modern man's impact on the environment is between ten and 100 times greater than it was in agrarian societies. In the long run, man will be able to survive on earth only insofar as he can respect the physico-chemical and biological limits that enable him to survive as a species. Three forms of logic operate here: global logic regulating the climate and dependent on biogeochemical, hydrological and oceanographic cycles; the logic of the ecosystems to which plants and animals belong; and the logic of the anthroposphere, regulated by the various types of society devised by human beings, each one with its own specific sociocultural structure, production pattern and environmental impacts. Population dynamics are part of that third logic: as Samuel Preston says, unlike all other species upon which biologists and ecologists have based their carrying capacity theory, 'man constructs his own environment',[15] from which he derives sustenance.

┌─ *In the news* ───┐

The High Price of Development in South-East Asia

The World Bank puts the cost of pollution and congestion in Jakarta at between $400 and $800 million a year, and at between 1 and 3 billion dollars in terms of medical care and loss of productivity in Bangkok... Energy demand is also increasing faster than economic growth, and the total number of cars is doubling on average every seven years, without any proper control of exhaust emissions... Within the space of a generation, the lifestyle and living conditions of tens of millions of people have been radically transformed: schooling, electricity, television, health services and finally, the consumer society. Urbanization is rampant and the main areas of development are increasingly voracious... In other words, if it is to protect its environment, South-East Asia should already start to consider diverting substantial resources even if this means accepting at least a temporary slowing down of its economic expansion.

Jean-Claude Pomonti, Le Monde, *March 1995, Paris*

└───┘

Discussion of the interrelationships between population growth and natural resources is often founded on the concept of carrying capacity. Virtually everyone agrees that there is an absolute global limit. On the basis of three elements – temperature, biomass and oxygen – Hubert Greppin puts it at somewhere between 10 and 30 billion human beings. More often than not, the relationship between population growth and resources is posited as an equation whose ideal outcome should be a balance between the two. A myth has thus been constructed of an optimal world population and past equilibria, none of which has ever actually existed. On the contrary, the history of population is replete with all sorts of crises and upheavals. The relationship between human beings and resources, or between mankind and nature, is first and foremost a dynamic relationship in which man redefines his place and the ways in which he relates to others. He does so on the basis of numerous factors, including available technology and the purpose he assigns to his actions. The idea that fertility reduction will necessarily foster environmental protection is short-sighted insofar as, given the lifestyle in the industrialized countries, the improved standard of living that supposedly accompanies a decline in fertility is more

61

Three Hundred Million Consumers

Would a visitor who strolled through Connaught Place, New Delhi's commercial district, five years ago recognize it today? This area, with its many colonial build-ings, is now showing the visible signs of ostentatious wealth... Of course, consumer appetite is not a recent phenomenon... But since economic reforms were initiated in 1991 this appetite has become frenzied... One million refrigerators have been sold, 250,000 washing machines, 912,000 scooters (there were 90,000 scooters on the road in 1972!), 10 million watches, 4.8 million television sets (the number of households hooked up to the cable network is put at 6 million)... 'If we succeed in increasing our current 5.5 per cent growth rate to 6 or 7 per cent over the next five years, we will be able to turn the population into one huge middle class of 550 million people — the world's biggest market!'

François Musseau, Libération, *February 1995, Paris*

likely to lead to increased consumption in the countries of the South. Initially, a greater environmental impact may be expected unless specific institutional, political and technological conditions are created to counter the effects of an improved standard of living in those countries.

The arguments used to justify the direction of action to combat poverty and environmental degradation have neglected institutions' role in the inter-actions between demographic, economic and environmental variables. However, without doubt one of the important achievements of the last decade has been the work done to highlight that role: social science research indicates that the relationships between population and development are regulated by social structure patterns and rules of economic and political behaviour.[16]

The Programme of Action attaches particular importance to providing food security, halting environmental degradation and combating poverty. These are discussed here as part of a broader approach aimed at identifying systemic relationships rather than limited causality, and elucidating the politi-cal and institutional framework within which action may be realistically envisaged. With regard to food, the United Nations Food and Agriculture Organization (FAO) indicates that it is technically possible to feed ten billion human beings. However, technical success criteria neglect the ecological impact of increased agricultural output as well as the importance of the sociopolitical and institutional realities determining access to food: produc-tion factors (land, water, fertilizers, credit etc.), funds for buying it, and the means of transporting and storing it.

Jean-Paul Porterie highlights below the gap between the technical aspect of food security and what is actually involved, i.e. meeting world food needs, particularly the needs of the poorest groups.

Feeding the People of Tomorrow: A Two-sided Problem
Jean-Paul Porterie

Both worldwide and in most developing countries, food supplies are now markedly better than they were 30 years ago, but not all social groups have benefited equitably from this improvement. What are the prospects for food in view of the inevitable population increase in the countries of the South and the disparity between the technical possibility of producing enough food to meet demand and the actual food access possibilities of a large part of the world population?

Increased Production is Technically Possible

The FAO says that if the growing food demand is to be met by 2010, agricultural output will have to be increased. Such an increase, it notes, will depend essentially on intensifying farming in the developing countries, i.e. improved yields, an increase in the total area under cultivation and irrigation, and more intensive use of available land (multiple harvests, a reduction in the amount of fallow land).[17]

Extension of cropland will be possible[18] only in those few areas where land is still available, i.e. Africa and Latin America and, to a lesser extent, East Asia. It will probably contribute to the deforestation of certain areas, although to what extent is difficult to estimate. The need for cropland will have to be met by increasing the intensity of crop growing – that is, increasing the number of harvests per year.[19]

Increases in productivity will depend to a large extent on maintaining and extending the irrigated sector, which will require about 20 per cent more surface area by 2010. This percentage marks a slowing of the expansion of irrigated cropland, which is inevitable owing to the rising unit costs of irrigation investment, the dwindling number of appropriate sites and water resources, and the need to avoid negative environmental impacts. Moreover, in addition to the investment needed for equipping new irrigated areas, investment will be required for rehabilitating land degraded by salination and waterlogging.

The use of fertilizers will have to be increased substantially to offset soil nutrient loss.[20] There are great regional disparities: whereas fertilizers are overused in some parts of the world, with consequent water and soil pollution, in Africa only 11 kilograms per hectare are used and even twice that amount would be insufficient to prevent nutrient depletion in some areas. Supply of the necessary quantities therefore seems unlikely without major technical problems, substantial price increases or unacceptable environmental impacts.

Meeting Populations' Needs is a Totally Different Matter

It should be borne in mind that the prospects for increased agricultural output described above relate to the possibility of meeting the food demand projected for the year 2010, and not to *how* to meet food needs. The projected level of demand is itself determined by hypotheses based on the increase in income during the period in question, which assume mediocre income growth prospects in the developing countries.[21] Therefore, this relatively optimistic prediction does not mean that the food situation will be satisfactory in 2010.

Food supplies for 1988–1990 have been put at 2700 calories per person per day worldwide, with substantial regional variations: in sub-Saharan Africa and South Asia supplies were respectively 2100 and 2200 calories per day,[22] compared with 3400 calories per day in the industrialized countries. Since the population increase rates forecast for the poorest regions are among the highest, it will be difficult to bring all countries up to levels of at least 3000 calories.

The FAO believes it is possible to increase the average daily amount to 2860 calories by 2010. Increases, however, would be very uneven: + 3 to 4 per cent in Africa and the Middle East, + 17 per cent in East Asia and + 10 per cent in the two other regions. Africa and South Asia would remain below the 3000 calories mark, and 637 million people (11 per cent of the population of the countries of the South) would still be chronically undernourished, including 300 million in Africa and 200 million in South Asia. In those circumstances, there is justification for believing that the 'meeting of demand' scenario would be a failure in terms of human needs.[23] A normative scenario, which examined the prospects for meeting needs rather than for achieving the output required to satisfy a theoretical solvent demand, would obviously give a completely different idea of the problems to be resolved as a matter of priority.

On the basis of the above figures, it is possible to calculate for the different regions of the world the food supply increase rates needed to achieve the 3100 calories average. This figure, the FAO projection for the Middle East and East Asia, is interesting because at that level the percentage of undernourished people is very low. In the demand-based scenario food supplies for sub-Saharan Africa would have to grow by 5 per cent a year instead of 3.3 per cent, i.e. a 50 per cent difference; for South Asia, by 3.6 per cent instead of 2.4 per cent, also a 50 per cent difference; and for Latin America and the Caribbean, by 2.4 per cent instead of 2.2 per cent. Clearly, in the normative scenario the production effort would encounter constraints made greater by their nature and intensity.

Restrictive Factors

In the FAO analysis, one of the main reasons for the difficulties in achieving more satisfactory consumption levels is the non-agricultural population's insufficient income, which prevents it from meeting its needs at the market price. Since technical production constraints would play only a minor role here, the failure of the 'meeting of demand' scenario referred to above would therefore be due rather to the non-agricultural sectors. Other sources, however, are pessimistic about agriculture's physical constraints.

In 1955, cultivated land per inhabitant in the countries of the South was 0.45 hectares. In 1990, it was no more than 0.21 hectares and in 2010 it will still probably have decreased by a quarter, down to 0.16 hectares. Agricultural land acquisition for expanding cities and infrastructures, the abandonment of worn out or polluted land and population growth are factors in this trend. Few countries have substantial land reserves. Available land, where it exists, is generally wooded and consequently the ecological disadvantages of clearing it are much more obvious than the advantages, especially in the long term.

Moreover, erosion and more generally soil degradation make usable land less productive. Human activities worldwide have degraded 17 per cent of land surface (deserts excluded) since 1945: the loss of humus, the deformation of the terrain, its salination and waterlogging affect more than a third of irrigated areas, with a considerable impact in terms of production shortfall and investment loss. Between 5 and 10 million hectares of arable and grazing land are abandoned every year, and much larger areas become more drought-prone and less productive.

In an even greater number of cases, the main restriction is a lack of water. The apparent abundance of water is deceptive: the usable proportion (renewable fresh water) is in fact only 0.0075 per cent, and often is not available where and when it is required. Furthermore, water transportation and conservation cause serious economic, health and environmental problems. Water is a finite resource and is very vulnerable in terms of its flows and chemical properties, which human activities can easily rarefy and pollute. Irrigated agriculture is currently the main user of water[24] and even moderate expansion rates in this sector generate substantial needs. Moreover, per capita needs for non-agricultural uses (industrial, domestic and municipal) are growing very rapidly because of urbanization and industrialization. Consequently, there will be fierce competition for water among different sectors, even outside the arid and semi-arid regions. The consequences can be dramatic: where local competition is intense owing to rapid urbanization, as in northern China, farmers have already been deprived of water – a new variant of the urban bias. Elsewhere, the development of large irrigated areas has ruined entire downstream regions, as in the case of the Aral Sea.

Concerted multisectoral strategies and appropriate price policies are needed to improve water use efficiency. Currently, water is often heavily subsidized, particularly water for irrigation purposes, and this encourages inefficient management and waste. Using projections for the population–water resources ratio,[25] we can already identify situations that will probably require painful adjustments before 2025: the North African countries, the Great Lakes and Horn of Africa region, the Arabian Peninsula and the Jordan River basin will have to radically overhaul not only their water supply systems but particularly their water use systems.[26]

The study of arid regions has tended to explain land degradation in terms of population growth. In Ronald Jaubert's opinion, however, more complex mechanisms underlie the process, particularly where nomadic populations are concerned. Population growth has played an upstream role by causing settled populations' land needs to increase. As far as nomads are concerned, he believes that the disruption of their environment's precarious balance is due first and foremost to the policies of states and the method of resource appropriation they have supported.

The Populations of the Arid Regions
Ronald Jaubert

Malthusian theories find a particular echo in regions prone to desertification (one-sixth of all land above water and approximately 900 million inhabitants). Repeated famines, resource degradation and a growing number of conflicts all tend to substantiate the theory of alarming overpopulation in regions least able to feed their people. The outside observer sees the unprecedented increase in food aid[27] as proof of this. However, careful analysis of societies in those regions reveals that their main problems stem not from population growth, but from marginalization, reduced living space and the plundering of resources over the last few decades. In fact, the semi-arid regions are one of those cropland extension areas referred to above. This extension process, which shows every sign of increasing in the coming years, thrusts the nomadic or semi-nomadic populations and their flocks into the least productive and most fragile regions. Bordering deserts, arid regions were once important trade routes: the trans-Saharan routes in Africa, and the Silk Road linking East and West through the Arabian Desert. But now they are nothing more than dead ends. The revolution in sea and land transport, however, was only one of the factors in isolating these populations: the main ones were political and economic.

Settlement Policies

Nomadic and semi-nomadic populations have long been regarded as archaic and destructive of their environment.[28] From the 1950s onwards and up until the 1980s, governments and international organizations endeavoured to settle nomads, arguing that they were both the first victims of resource degradation and also those primarily responsible for it. Hardin[29] played an important role at the end of the 1960s in justifying settlement policies on the grounds that the collective ownership of pastureland is incompatible with sound management (or 'sustainable' management, as we would say today) of pastoral resources. Thus, only the state is truly capable of managing collective resources.

That view, widely shared by the leaders of the Sahel, North African and Middle Eastern states, helped to justify, among other things, the use of coercive policies against nomadic populations, which were generally outside the control of the new independent states. The social organization of nomadic and semi-nomadic societies was often seen as an opposition force structuring a politically unreliable popula- tion. The primary aim of settlement programmes and attempts to control pastoral resource use was to strengthen state control over these populations. The latent conflict between the authorities and populations with little or no official representa- tion had serious consequences in the Sahel, particularly the delay in acknowledging the drought that began in the early 1970s. Its belated recognition was due to the fact that the nomads were the first population group affected. Governments did not acknowledge the ensuing famine until the settled populations were affected. Although a USAID report in 1970 put the number of people in need of emergency food aid at over three million, significant relief efforts and dispatch of aid did not start until 1973. This delay cost a considerable number of lives.

In the news

Kenya: Trees are on the March?

Between the years 1986 and 1992, Kenya had probably the fastest growing popu- lation in the world, increasing by 4 per cent per year. Yet a survey by Swedish scientists, covering regions of the country which hold a total of 80 per cent of the Kenyan population, has found that there has been, 'contrary to prevailing beliefs, a rapid increase of planted woody biomass'.

During the six years of the study, when Kenya's population grew by about 24 per cent, the standard volume of planted trees grew by more than 30 per cent... Meanwhile, the amount of natural vegetation remains 'approximately constant'.

The conventional view is that in most of Africa, people are stripping the land of wood to burn as fuel. It has been assumed that more people mean greater destruc- tion – leading to the spread of deserts. [Peter] Holmgren's study found the opposite: 'Instead of increasing fuelwood deficit, Kenyan farmers seem to apply wise and sustainable management practices, including tree growing.' [Likewise] in Senegal, reports of a fuelwood crisis resulted from a 'total misreading of the situation by outside experts'. Natural forests were being replaced by farm forests and there was no shortage of fuelwood.

Fred Pearce, New Scientist, *24/31 December 1994, London*

The problem took on an international dimension only because of media coverage of the drought's social consequences. In 1974 the United Nations decided to hold an international conference on its impacts. The conference, which took place in 1977, focused on the environmental impacts and the risk of desertification rather than on the problems of the arid regions' inhabitants. The human catastrophe, the way the drought had been managed and its other aspects were largely neglected. Consequently, the plan of action adopted by the conference was very limited in scope, including at the strictly environmental level. In 1992, a study by the United Nations Environment Programme concluded that soil and vegetation degradation had worsened.[30] Moreover, the marginalization of the arid regions' populations and, in many parts, their growing impoverishment had by no means been halted.[31] The countries concerned had other priorities. Over the period 1978–1983 less than a third of the funds for implementing the desertification action plan in the countries of the Sahel was used for rural development. Of the funds actually allocated to rural development, more than 30 per cent were used for export crops. Improved cattle-breeding accounted for approximately 5 per cent of aid. Programmes focused mainly on technical improvements, to the detriment of central issues such as forms of resource management and organization of production.

The policies of the last two decades have helped thrust nomadic populations into low-productivity areas. Cropland has been extended in the Sahel and also in India and the Middle East, thus disadvantaging pastureland. This has exacerbated tensions between populations benefiting from investments and those that have been left out. In Senegal, for example, the development of irrigated perimeters has led to a substantial decrease in grazing land on river banks. This land was a particularly important fodder reserve in drought years. The clashes at the end of the 1980s between Mauritanian cattle-breeders and Senegalese farmers were the direct result of competition for the control of land included in the water-resource development programme.

Rio: a New Approach Idealizes Traditional Solidarity

The Rio Conference marked a clear change in attitudes, strongly emphasizing as it did the need to increase populations' participation in development activities, particularly through the revival of local knowledge and traditional resource management structures. A similar line was taken in the International Convention to Combat Desertification, in the preamble to which populations are one of the main concerns. In addition, the World Bank recently published two studies on participation and traditional land systems. Progress, therefore, has definitely been made, and the strategies proposed are certainly more attractive than coercive policies. They are based, however, more on an idealized view of nomadic societies than on an accurate factual assessment, and to that extent they limit the convention's chances of success. The convention, moreover, has two major weaknesses.

State control of resource management has been very largely a failure.[32] Replacing it overnight by traditional community forms of management would be to ignore fifty years of profound changes in societies and their physical environment. What is left of community solidarity? What is the role of so-called traditional structures in regulating production systems? Although there may be no answers to those questions, traditional solidarity as it existed fifty years ago can be said to belong to a past which in many cases has gone for ever. Today aid allocation is dependent on setting up local organizations: this makes the idea of traditional solidarity completely artificial.[33] Many such organizations are set up either to meet aid criteria or to manage funds received. They often last no longer than the project itself. What is more, these so-called grass-roots organizations are set up for projects such as building a dispensary, market-garden production and anti-erosion work. The hallmark of such activities is that they are carried out in small, clearly defined areas. They are therefore totally different from the approach appropriate to arid-region resource management, which must extend beyond local matters.

Another Method of Resource Management

The future of arid regions' populations depends partly on redefining resource exploitation methods. Their active participation may alter resource distribution, but when resources are deemed to be of crucial national importance, there is little likelihood of their being allocated to the inhabitants of regions regarded as marginal. Governments' support for strategies based on consolidating local structures is probably less an expression of their desire to put in place this model proposed by the countries of the North than of their relative loss of sovereignty. The International Convention to Combat Desertification provides that states have the sovereign right to exploit their own resources in accordance with their own environment and development policy. In view of the financial and food shortfalls in most of those countries of the South to which the convention relates, it is unlikely that the policies for exploiting arid-region resources (water, mineral or tourism-related) can be radically overhauled. A participatory approach, and use of non-governmental organizations and traditional structures provide a useful alternative in a period of structural adjustment. In fact, they help to justify the inevitable withdrawal of government structures. The approaches proposed by the Rio Conference will have to contend with economic constraints and the need for increased agricultural output. In addition, they risk being confined to regions with the least potential.

Chapter 4

The Gaps in the Programme of Action

The third major set of topics in the Programme of Action comprises those issues that were scarcely dealt with in the negotiations – general mortality, ageing and migration. This is indicative of the scant attention paid to the specific demographic dimension of current developments, and to their origins and political repercussions. Mortality, its causes, socioeconomic differentiation factors and dramatic increase in parts of the world were passed over in silence. Elderly people were dealt with only superficially, despite the importance attached to them by the Asian countries at their regional conference. Migration is in the Programme of Action because it is unavoidable, but governments endeavoured to make as few commitments as possible. The recommendations on these three topics are summarized below.

Mortality, Ageing and Migration: Programme of Action

Mortality

The availability, accessibility, acceptability and affordability of health-care facilities and services for all people must be improved. Governments must endeavour to increase the lifespan and quality of life and reduce disparities in life expectancy between and within countries.

All countries should reduce mortality and morbidity and aim to achieve by 2005 a life expectancy at birth greater than 70 years and by 2015 a life expectancy at birth greater than 75 years. Governments should ensure community participation in health policy planning and aim to make basic health-care services more financially sustainable.

Elderly People

The steady increase in the number of elderly people is fraught with consequences in most industrialized and developing countries. Economically and socially, this increase is both an opportunity and a challenge.

All countries must therefore develop health-care systems as well as economic and social security systems, paying special attention to women's needs. These systems must be based on intergenerational equity and solidarity. Governments must encourage multigenerational families and establish formal and informal family-based support systems for elderly people. At the same time they should strive to enable elderly people to remain independent, healthy and productive as long as possible or as desired, and to make full use of their skills and abilities for the benefit of society. The valuable contribution that elderly people make to families and society, especially as volunteers and care-givers, should be given due recognition and encouragement.

Migration

Three main steps should be taken. Migration flows should be reduced and the root political and economic causes should be dealt with; the management of 'controlled migrations' should be improved for the mutual benefit of the countries concerned; and states' rights to limit migration should be made compatible with individuals' rights to freedom of movement.

International migration is affected by economic imbalances, poverty and environmental degradation, combined with the absence of peace and security, human rights violations and the varying degrees of development of judicial and democratic institutions. In recent years, 1.4 million people have migrated, two-thirds of them from developing countries. It is the right of every nation state to decide who can enter and stay in its territory. Such right, however, should be exercised taking care to avoid racist or political actions. Countries must ratify the International Convention on the Protection of Migrants and identify strategies to ensure that migration contributes to development. Orderly migration can have positive impacts on both the countries of origin and the countries of destination.

The manageability of migration hinges on making the option to remain in one's country a viable one for all people; managing international migration flows transparently; adopting monetary policies and providing banking facilities that enable the safe and timely transfer of migrants' funds; entering into bilateral or multilateral agreements to improve migrants' skills within the framework of certain forms of temporary migration; safeguarding the rights and wages of migrants; and promoting the return of migrants on a voluntary basis and their reintegration into their home countries.

Countries must facilitate the economic integration and social protection of documented migrants; consider granting such migrants civil and political rights and responsibilities, and facilitating their naturalization; eliminate discriminatory practices directed against them; protect them against racism; and guarantee respect for their cultural and religious values. Furthermore, countries must recognize the vital importance of the family unit and integrate this concept into their legislation so as to guarantee the protection of these migrants' family unity.

Countries must address the root causes of undocumented migration, prevent all international trafficking in undocumented migrants and punish those who organize it. Furthermore, they should discourage such migration by making potential migrants aware of the entry, residence and employment conditions imposed by host countries.

In less than 10 years the number of refugees has more than doubled, from 8.5 to 19 million. Most have sought refuge in developing countries, thus imposing burdens which their economies are unable to bear. An increase in movements is likely, particularly of refugees and undocumented migrants. It is therefore necessary to reduce pressures responsible for such movements by taking preventive measures, combating the root causes and endeavouring to find durable solutions to the plight of displaced persons. Protection should be ensured to refugees, the erosion of the institution of asylum should be prevented, and refugee assistance programmes should be integrated into development planning with due attention to gender equity.

General Mortality

The considerable life expectancy differences throughout the world called for a thorough analysis of mortality differential factors. The same is true of health differences which, although less statistically visible, are equally dramatic. The precarious living conditions of large population segments in almost all countries, together with widespread political, socioeconomic and environmental crises, impact directly on people's physical and mental ability to lead healthy and productive lives.

Although the inhabitants of the industrialized countries can aspire to enjoying their full biological lifespan and reaching the age of natural death without repeated illnesses and chronic physical deterioration, that is not so for most of mankind. Recent data reveal the regression of health indicators in a number of countries, particularly in central and eastern Europe, as well as the persistence of easily preventable diseases or even an upsurge in them. The Programme of Action attaches importance to maternal, infant and sexuality-related mortality (AIDS), but unfortunately neglects adult mortality (other than maternal mortality). A human-centred approach to development emphasizing 'human capital' would have required a more thorough analysis of mortality and morbidity, because these provide a clearer indication of different social groups' living conditions than do fertility levels.

In the news

The Russian People Threatened with Disaster

Radioactive waste hurriedly buried, groundwater contaminated, forests decimated – a report by the Security Council of the Russian Federation paints an apocalyptic picture of the former USSR's natural resource situation. And it predicts that the population will degenerate over the next 50 years. 'If we regard mankind as the primary indicator of environmental degradation, then the catastrophe has already occurred, and it is a sizeable one', says Professor Alexei Yablokov, a biologist at the Academy of Sciences, who presided over the Council's work. 'Life expectancy is declining, diseases are on the increase and there are a growing number of birth defects', he adds, waving a report about a mysterious form of jaundice in the Altai Mountains region, supposedly linked to nuclear pollution, which affects 40 per cent of newborn babies. Russian male life expectancy fell from 64 years in 1985 to 58 years in 1993 – figures similar to those for Kenya or Indonesia.

Luc Perrot, Libération, February 1995, Paris

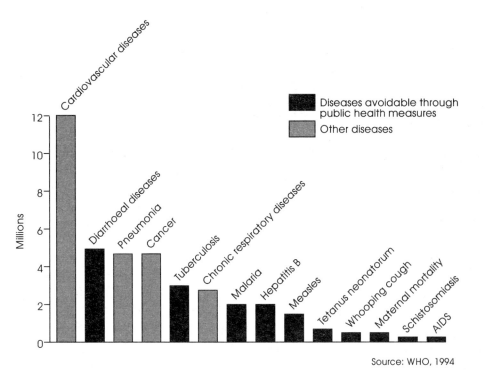

Source: WHO, 1994

Figure 4.1 *Causes of Mortality in the World, 1992*

73

Population Ageing

The delegations to the Cairo Conference agreed that population ageing is not a problem in itself, but represents a new challenge. It prompts a reassessment of health and social security policies, and elderly people themselves are a source of knowledge and experience which societies could put to better use.

An Inevitable and General Trend

Ageing is an unavoidable issue for two reasons. First, it is inevitable and will affect people in all societies sooner or later. Consequently, population growth and ageing are the two dimensions of one and the same phenomenon, a sudden decline in population growth causing ageing to accelerate. Second, ageing presents each country with particular challenges. In industrialized countries, the challenge is one of intergenerational relationships (human relationships but also social security systems) and the choice between endeavouring to prolong life as much as possible and ensuring an old age of quality for the vast majority of people.

In the countries of the South, the challenges relate particularly to global strategies. For example, rapid fertility reduction due to a voluntary-based policy leads to more rapid population ageing. An alternative strategy might be a better spread of efforts over time so as to retain greater latitude for finding suitable institutional, human and economic solutions. There is a major problem for the countries of the South: the lack of a social welfare system due to the fact that elderly people have hitherto been looked after mainly by their families.

A population ages when people's average age increases. Between 1950 and 1970 the median age, i.e. the age dividing the population into two quantitatively equal groups, fell worldwide from 23.4 to 21.6 years. Since 1970, the trend has reversed and the median age is once again what it was in 1950. With the continuing decline in fertility and mortality, the median age may be approximately 31.2 years in 2025. 'The whole world grew younger from 1950 to 1970 because of the substantial fall in infant mortality. Since 1985, it has steadily aged because of the great decline in fertility simultaneously in the industrialized and the developing countries. The sole exception is Africa, which has continued to grow younger.'[1] The ageing of a population's structure is very much part of the pattern of demographic change. Some people refer to this phenomenon as a second transition accompanying the changes in the economic system and the social structure, just as the decline in fertility accompanied the industrialization and modernization of Western agricultural economies.

Bottom-up ageing is due to the decline in fertility, which decreases the relative proportion of those under 15 years of age in the overall population. In

1975, 43 per cent of the inhabitants of South Asia and Latin America were under the age of 15; in 2025, the figure will be only 25 per cent. Top-down ageing is linked to a decline in mortality, which increases the number of people over the age of 65 in the overall population.

Ageing in those countries of the South where there has been rapid population growth in recent decades will be particularly marked owing to the abrupt decline in fertility. China is an excellent illustration in this respect: the proportion of persons over 65, currently just under 10 per cent of the total population, will rise to about 22 per cent within 50 years. In terms of absolute numbers, this means that the number of people over 65 will have increased from 50 to 280 million between 1980 and 2050 (a multiplying factor of five to seven). China is a significant example for other countries of the South. The Chinese demographer I. Chuan Beyens Wu[2] believes that because of its birth control policy the country is faced with a dilemma that will inevitably be faced by all countries seeking to reduce their fertility rate as quickly as possible.

If they are to cope with population ageing, individuals and social institutions alike require an extraordinary ability to adapt within an extremely short space of time. In China, social policy makes families responsible for looking after elderly people. The 1980 marriage law provides that children are obliged to take care of their maternal and paternal parents. At the turn of the century, an elderly parent will be cared for by approximately four children, but as of 2030 only two or fewer children will be caring for an elderly parent. Will Chinese society, one wonders, be able to cope with this new situation? If so, how will it cope? Several Chinese demographers have drawn attention to this issue, arguing that fertility reduction targets should be reconsidered in the light of fertility's impact on ageing.

The Challenges of Ageing

The response to ageing depends first and foremost on the approach to it. At the individual level, ageing is an entirely relative concept. Physiologically speaking, the age of 65 at which, by convention, working life ends and retirement begins is quite arbitrary. This age has varied over the centuries. The French statesman Colbert introduced the age criterion in the seventeenth century to divide the population into two groups – those who could bear arms and the rest. He set the age at 60, and this remained unchanged up until the end of the nineteenth century. The concept of retirement has existed since the middle of the eighteenth century; it referred to the impossibility of continuing to earn one's living because of physical decline and age-related incapacities.[3] This clear break between the individual's biological age and social age may be said to have created old age.

┌─ *In the news* ───┐

China: The Grandfather Trap

China is growing old. More than that, it is growing old faster than any society in history. A process that took 85 years in Sweden and 32 years in Japan will take only 21 years in China, according to the Beijing Centre of Gerontology. Because of its size alone, China already has the largest number of elderly in the world...

According to the Chinese Statistics Bureau, in 1991, the proportion of people over the age of 60 to those between the ages of 15 and 60 was only 13.5% ... it leaps dramatically to 23.8% in 2020, 36% in 2030, and a whopping 44.9% in 2050 – with more than 400 million people over 60 years of age. That means that there will be almost one retired person for every two workers.

William McGurn, Far Eastern Economic Review,
December 1994, Hong Kong

The reality of ageing lies not so much in the increased average lifespan (expressed in terms of life expectancy) as in the fact that ageing is becoming democratic, i.e. more and more people are reaching old age. Consequently, there is now a new period of life between retirement age and the age at which physical deterioration begins, which is known as the threshold of dependency. Ageing is a problem if elderly people are regarded as burdens incapable of contributing to society. It is also a problem if a static perspective is adopted; that is, if current economic and social structures are projected into the future. However, facts show that everything is changing and that a linear perspective prevents us from realizing the extraordinary diversity of changes underway both in social values and practices and among institutions regulating relations between individuals and the State.

People aged over 65 in 1990 were born before 1925 and those who are currently children will turn 65 in 2050. Between the first and last dates, there will have been progress in terms of standard of living, hygiene, food, medicine, gynaecology and obstetrics. Individual behaviour, habits, career patterns and significant moments in life (marriage, motherhood, beginning of working life, divorce etc.) are changing rapidly. As a result, the elderly people of tomorrow will probably be much better equipped to live out their old age to the full than are today's people over 65, particularly in the industrialized countries, i.e. those countries that have benefited most from the period since 1925. Changes in women's activities, for example, and the impact on their health suggest that life-expectancy differences between men and women could decrease. If that is so, elderly women will probably not always outnumber elderly men.

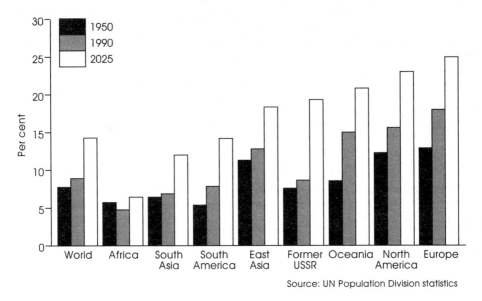

Figure 4.2 *Proportion of the Population Aged 60 and Over in 1950 and 1990, with predicted figures for 2025*

Furthermore, since industrialized countries' economies are increasingly composed of service activities, and since work methods are changing, it is quite foreseeable that retirement itself will mean something totally different in the near future. Finally, although there will always be very old people in poor health who are utterly dependent on material and human help in their daily lives, this stage is becoming increasingly short. Properly prepared for, individually and socially, old age can open up new prospects for living out a full biological lifespan, resulting in an extraordinary improvement in quality of life.

The Need to Make Social Choices

In the industrialized countries life expectancy at birth has increased by six years over the last quarter-century. Expectation of healthy life, on the other hand, appears to have remained constant at about 58 years for men and 63 years for women, although experts are not fully agreed about the criteria for this type of expectancy. Age is particularly relevant as a deterioration and dependence indicator. Instead of being defined in terms of the number of years lived, the beginning of old age may be defined on the basis of the number of years still to be lived, the age at which ten more years of life remain being taken as the age at which deterioration starts. In France this age was 64 years in 1750, 66.4 years in 1900, 71 years in 1957 and 75 years in 1985.[4]

According to Jacques Légaré,[5] the concept of expectation of healthy life will become increasingly important. This is because of the inevitable debate on the implications of longevity, and particularly on the choice between prolonging life as long as possible (haven't some people said that life expectancy could be increased to 100 or even 120 years?) and providing the largest possible number of people with a life of quality and dignity up until a reasonable age. The response to this dilemma depends on the type of society in question. From the sociological viewpoint and from that of individual quality of life, old age raises numerous questions which vary from one society to another, according to each country's economic and sociocultural parameters. In the industrialized countries, particular areas of concern are the perception of old age, its values and portrayals; elderly people's status and social function; retirement and health-care funding; the medicalization of old age and death; the definition of at-risk groups; self-reliance (i.e. individual judgment and the ability to take personal decisions alone); independence (i.e. the ability to carry out unaided the activities of daily living); care and aid structures; intergenerational transfers; and multigenerational relations. Solutions to these problems will determine social cohesion, the place of the elderly in public life, and the dignity and degree of well-being that societies will be able to ensure for a growing proportion of their population.

In the opinion of Hermann-Michel Hagmann, the future of retirement schemes and intergenerational relations depends on the way societies deal with

> 'the intergenerational division of labour; harmonization of shortened working life with increased expectation of healthy life; reconciliation of retirement scheme funding (members' increasing longevity) with company employment policy (shorter careers); decompartmentalization of training, work and leisure periods throughout the individual life cycle; the quest for a society with full employment and/or a full range of activities for people of all ages so as to create a meaningfulness transcending the market economy and develop socially useful activities; and replacement of a dependence-based approach by one highlighting intergenerational interdependence.'[6]

Because demographic changes are occurring at different rates, we need to adopt a comparative approach to have an idea of what the future holds in store for the world's populations. In the short and medium terms, the countries of the North will be more profoundly affected by those changes than the countries of the South. The latter, however, will be affected more rapidly than the industrialized countries. Furthermore, the rural areas will be more affected than the urban areas since internal migrants are generally young people. According to Dominique Tabutin,[7] the situation of the countries of the South gives much cause for concern. The ageing of the European populations certainly presents many challenges, but it has occurred in relatively favourable circumstances. For example, there has been economic growth, an increase in living standards and widespread employment; there is a social welfare system offering various benefits; and health services have been improved. European societies have thus enjoyed unprecedented economic and social development, even though demographically they began to decline at the beginning of this century.

In the news

'Elderly Person, Living Alone, Offers Room to Student (Male or Female)'

Elderly person seeks student for company and to share accommodation. Just over two years ago the University of Granada started an intergenerational shared accommodation programme, which has now been adopted by at least seven other Spanish universities. This solidarity-based exchange of services has proved very fruitful... 'I enrolled in this programme out of solidarity with young people, but also because I wanted to have someone to talk to when things are difficult', says Lourdes Lopez-Mateos. 'My daughter works a lot. She wanted me to hire a mature woman to look after me. But when I heard about this programme, I requested a student without asking my children's opinion'... A person offering an apartment is almost always a woman over 70, who can manage on her own and has a monthly income of under 50,000 pesetas [approximately US$ 384]. She particularly wants company and help with everyday jobs... The typical student is aged between 20 and 24, and in 77 per cent of cases is female... Students enrol in the programme for financial reasons, and sometimes also because they want to show solidarity with elderly people. In exchange, the universities or institutions participating in the programme give the students help with buying books or meals... Although originally designed as a way of solving student accommodation problems, this initiative is actually much broader in scope.

Alejandro V. García, El País, February 1995, Madrid

All this is very different from the situation in many countries of the South. After solid progress in terms of health indicators, disparities in wealth and inequalities between rural and urban areas are on the increase. Even in cities there are two types of individual: salary and wage earners, who have access to a social welfare system; and the majority, whose lives are extremely precarious. These people work in the informal economy and have only their daily earnings to count on. In most of the countries of the South, social security systems are either non-existent or only in their early stages, and health programmes cannot even meet the needs of adults and young people. Major economic and institutional obstacles prevent society from functioning properly and hinder any improvement in the lives of the elderly. Moreover, people's way of thinking is not prepared for the tasks ahead and there is a lack of awareness on the part of political decision-makers, who think only of short-term management.

In both the South and the North, governments are increasingly appealing to family solidarity to ensure material security for elderly people. In the industrialized countries a substantial number of men and women will be childless. In countries of the South with a one-child policy, many elderly people will also be alone and will have no help from their families. States, required to compensate for the lack of offspring of a significant part of their population, will have to take full account of the precarious situation caused by very low fertility. An additional problem will be elderly people who have children but who have, for various reasons, been abandoned by their families.

In the South, in addition to a decrease in the number of children, there are the effects of the erosion of traditional solidarity due to the economic crisis and changes in attitudes. Should current socioeconomic conditions persist, families will be unable to look after their 'old people'. Even in industrialized countries, family solidarity can have only a secondary effect. 'Modernity' means greater individual independence in relation to the family. At the same time, however, other forms of solidarity are growing up among neighbours, friends or more distant relatives – an example of the positive changes underway. In addition, a new form of intergenerational solidarity is developing, illustrated by the Spanish universities' shared accommodation programme described above. New forms of interpersonal ties are taking shape. These are based on elective relationships whereby help is given to an elderly person not because it is a family obligation, but either because there is a sense of responsibility in general or because there is an emotional bond with a specific person.

The Challenges of Migration

International Migration

The Cairo draft programme of action proposed introduction of the 'right to family reunification' in order to improve migrants' lives, but this was rejected by the industrialized countries. A compromise solution replacing that concept by the 'migrants' right to have a family life' also failed to meet with their approval. Despite protests by Mexico, Chile and China, the countries of the North agreed to endorse only a vague wording about 'the vital importance of family reunification'. The international migration debate did not make any further headway. Frustrated and unable to break the resistance of the countries of immigration, a number of delegations – on behalf of the countries of the South – called for an international migration conference. So far, however, the principle of this conference has still not been accepted by the United Nations General Assembly, the only body able to convene such a conference.

Like other international or regional fora, the Cairo Conference revealed governments' reluctance to discuss international migration in a multilateral setting. Migration is most definitely a troublesome issue: 'It is troublesome in the country of departure because it is tantamount to voting with one's feet – an adverse judgment passed on a dictatorship or on the incompetence of a system'.[8] It is also troublesome in countries of immigration, because of the growing cultural distance between nationals and immigrants at a time of unemployment and increasing lack of job security.

There are two main lessons to be drawn from the non-debate on migration. First, the situation needs to be downplayed through the dissemination of accurate information about the true extent of migration flows. Second, migration needs to be understood as an adaptation mechanism that should form an integral part of inter-state relations and international negotiations. Europe itself has made wide use of migration to solve the population growth and unemployment problems arising from radical economic changes. Between 1860 and 1914, more than 50 million Europeans migrated to the New World. Today many countries of the South have the same problems as Europe had during that period. This obliges the industrialized countries ethically and politically to include migration in their dialogue with the countries of the South. Furthermore, although development in the South will eventually mean that there are fewer reasons for migrating, substantial migration seems inevitable for the foreseeable future.

The Cairo Programme of Action distinguishes between documented and undocumented migrants, refugees, displaced persons, asylum seekers, individuals, families, men and women, temporary and permanent migrants, and potential and actual migration. These distinctions are relevant as far as the strict regulation of migration is concerned. In the current international situation, migration is not only increasing but also taking considerably more complex forms. Given the globalization of trade, increased migration seems quite logi-

The World is Shrinking: Not Even Africa Wants
its Immigrants Any More

Boats in the Gulf of Guinea, their holds filled with migrants... A taxiplane offload-
ing in Lagos, Bamako, Dakar and Abidjan its cargo of emigrants expelled from
Zambia. Yesterday it was Nigeria, today it is Zambia, Gabon, South Africa. Africa is
barricading itself in, just like the European Union. And just like America, keeping
out the Mexicans, Haitians and Cubans... One person in 115 is a refugee, someone
who has had to leave his or her country for economic, military or political reasons...
At the Cairo Conference ... the countries of the North refused to accept the right
to family reunification. Their borders will be open only to those they are prepared to
accept, i.e. very few people and quality migrants... Given the obstacles put in place
by the North, and the barriers erected by Gabon and South Africa, we may ask
ourselves whether migration is still a survival strategy... The migration issue is a
complex one in Africa, as elsewhere in the world. It cannot be resolved by receiving
countries' decrees or by a laissez-faire policy in the countries of departure. The fate
of migrants is certainly worth an international get-together, like the one in Cairo
last September.

El Bachir Sow, Le Soleil, *February 1995, Dakar*

cal. 'In 1990, migrant labour income was put at $50 billion compared with $5
billion in 1970 and $35 billion at the beginning of the 1980s. This reflects not
only workers' growing mobility but also the increase in the qualification level
of migrant manpower (technicians, executives, engineers).'[9]

Far from being a new phenomenon, migration has long been a means of
adapting to changes underway in survival and production systems all over the
world. 'In the history of the West, emigration has been both a safety valve in
times of pressure on the essentials of life, and an outlet for excess population
that has long served as a substitute for fertility control.'[10] The migration
debate in the Inter-Parliamentary Union earlier this century, outlined briefly
below, is a good illustration of this phenomenon.

At the 22nd Inter-Parliamentary Conference, held in Bern in 1924,
Senator Fernand-Merlin, the President of the French Inter-Parliamentary
Group, set out the situation as follows:

'The problem of emigration and immigration is a prime international concern.
One thing is certain: we cannot abandon to fate the material and spiritual
living conditions of thousands of human beings who have chanced to be born in
lands unable to feed their own populations... The ideal solution would be to

achieve an orderly and as precise as possible distribution of individuals and families, with a healthy and dignified life for everyone, particularly outside their own country... Population shifts will continue to grow because of the high birth rate in some countries and the need to spread excess population beyond their borders.'[11]

Because of their reluctance, the Union suggested to its members in 1928 that they propose to their parliaments that migration restrictions be abolished and bilateral agreements concluded with countries willing to accept migrants. The framework of this policy was quite clear: the migration problem was formulated in terms of combating unemployment; unemployment had to be remedied and employment opportunities had to be created throughout the world. Remedies envisaged by Inter-Parliamentary Conferences included a reduction in working time and major public works.[12] It is clear from the discussions that practical solutions to unemployment could not be sought solely within a national framework or in measures of limited scope, however effective and useful these might be.

During the inter-war period, two regions and one country regarded themselves as overpopulated: Europe, the Far East and India. Their members of Parliament wanted mass migration to be organized within the framework of inter-state agreements. They called for the creation of an international labour supermarket that would enable them to resettle their excess populations in overseas countries, with protection for their interests and rights. Jiuji Kasai, the Japanese delegate to the 1936 Budapest Conference, championed that viewpoint:

'Japan feels the strong pressure of her increasing population, which is growing at a rate of over one million people a year. Hence Japan must prepare to feed this increasing population... But already great nations have closed their doors to Japanese immigration... They must either open their gates to immigration or allot ... some of their territories.'[13]

It is for the reader to judge the significance of the word 'must'!

The debate started up again in 1954 in the context of the first World Population Congress, held in Rome. The Inter-Parliamentary Conference after the congress put mass migration back on the agenda. Since Europe's demographic situation had changed substantially between 1936 and 1955, and since economic development prospects were becoming increasingly real, European members of Parliament adopted more nuanced positions: as far as Europe was concerned, substantial emigration combined with a natural slowing of population growth and with economic development could, it was believed, ease demographic pressure. Some delegates still believed, however, that there was unused land – in Africa, for example – which emigrants could develop. It was during this period that the representatives of the non-Western countries began to make their voices heard. For example, an Iraqi member of Parliament observed that manpower movements of this sort were economically unsound because they were based on the incorrect assumption that there was work for immigrants in the countries of the South. A Sudanese member of Parliament was greatly concerned that immigrants behaved like conquerors, who tended to drive the indigenous population out of public life. A view especially prevalent in international discussions and debates during this period was that colonization was justified by the notion that there were overpopulated countries with the necessary tools for achieving progress and other countries empty and just waiting to be developed.

International migration nowadays is very different from what it was at the beginning of the century. Just about all available space is occupied and few countries, at least in the West, need additional manpower to help run their economies – quite the opposite, in fact. Migration continues nevertheless, and people such as Joaquín Arango argue that it is a fundamental trend for which there is only one realistic solution: accepting that it will continue and learning to cope with it from the viewpoint of its being the greatest possible benefit for all concerned.

Migration is Here to Stay
Joaquín Arango

The human species is a migratory species. Fear of migration is a recurring phenomenon which is now so great that one may legitimately speak of migration psychosis. In recent years, migration has become a politically sensitive issue because it is often linked, although not actively, with the rise of the extreme right. Current attitudes reveal that the size of migration flows has been overestimated and that there is great apprehension about their growth. There are three major errors in these attitudes. First, the doomsayers' argument is based on a mechanical extrapolation of the economic and demographic disparities between rich and poor nations. Consequently, they predict that the 'poor' are about to emigrate in large numbers to the countries of the North. Second, observers fail to take account of the political ability of countries of immigration to regulate entry. Third, when ways of lessening emigration incentives are considered, there is a tendency to exaggerate the effects of development as regards the countries of origin, and the potential effect of international cooperation on development. These errors prevent an understanding of the difference between potential and actual migration.

┌─ In the news ───┐

The Return of the Nomadic Scientists

In 1991, Colciencias established a network of foreign-based Colombian scientists to promote the creation and international exchange of scientific projects. It now has about a thousand members in nineteen countries. Then someone had the idea of helping those who wanted to return to Colombia to do so... Javier Narvaez, who has a doctorate in molecular physiology, is now coordinator of the national biotechnologies programme at the Colombian National Centre for Agronomic Research...

'My wife and I were working near Washington when in 1993 Corpoica, then being set up, proposed that we work on this programme. I think it is an excellent way of encouraging a large number of scientists to return to Colombia... The country is currently having great difficulty in finding the qualified staff it needs'... All these scientists are delighted that someone in Colombia had the idea of bringing them back. They are thus able to contribute their knowledge, and are very pleased they decided to return. They all agree, however, that the financial part of the programme must be made more flexible: they had to wait six months before they received the settling-in grants they had been promised. But they have absolutely no regrets about anything.

Semana, June 1994, Bogotá

└───┘

The fear inspired by current migration flows is not at all justified by their magnitude. There are now approximately 1.5 million migrants worldwide, two-thirds of whom are from the countries of the South. Migration flows from those countries have predominated only since the 1970s. Proper migration systems have been created through the establishment of preferential relations between countries of origin and destination. There are three main destinations – North America, Western Europe and the Asia-Pacific region. Another destination is the oil-producing Gulf states, which are a special case. In most countries of destination, there is no migrant employment policy. In the past, however, those countries had a proper recruitment policy and migration therefore met manpower needs. Because of the high unemployment in industrialized countries,[14] migration's political costs outweigh its economic advantages. Furthermore, new forms of migration now exist, mostly asylum requests, family reunification and illegal migration resulting from a breach of entry procedures.

There are two reasons for the deep concern about migration and the increasingly widespread policies restricting freedom of movement. The first of these is the enormous disparity between the migration potential of the countries of origin and the absorption capacity of the countries of destination. Migration potential is defined as the amount of emigration that would occur solely as a result of prevailing economic and social forces, without any political obstacles to freedom of movement. The second reason is the growing cultural differences between migrants and the populations of the countries of arrival. In Europe's case there is another important factor –

85

the way migration is perceived. Unlike North America and Australia, which were built on a positive view of immigration, European countries throughout history have been countries of emigration. They regard themselves today as complete, fully developed and ethnically homogeneous societies, and are therefore afraid that immigration will destroy their social cohesion.

Migration flows are commonly perceived as being like water in fluid mechanics, and it is considered inevitable that population disparities between adjoining regions automatically lead to a new geographical population distribution. This sort of logic applied to migration is completely wrong: the differences in population numbers are scarcely relevant in themselves; what count are population trends. Even so, because individual behaviour is neither linear nor automatic, it is difficult to make any predictions. For example, countries with the highest emigration rates do not have the highest birth or growth rates. Similarly, countries of immigration do not necessarily have a manpower shortage because of a low fertility rate and an ageing population. Popular opinion fantasizes about increased migration for two reasons. First, it forgets that countries have borders and therefore relatively effective means of legal dissuasion. Second, contrary to the prevailing theory that people have a chronic tendency to migrate, empirical observation indicates that human beings have been very much inclined to stay in their own countries, except in a number of very specific historical periods.

However, although the predicted large-scale emigration will almost certainly not occur, problems will not go away. The present situation will persist because there is no sign of any major change in its parameters in the near future. It has adverse consequences for the countries of emigration: migration restrictions deprive them of a valve for removing socioeconomic pressures as well as of sources of income, both once available to the industrialized countries. The situation has similar consequences for countries of immigration where there are social tensions originating elsewhere. The South's greater than ever migration potential stems from many factors: social upheavals and dislocation due to the development process; the continuing economic crisis and the social effects of structural adjustment; population growth increasing the demand for goods, services and jobs; the attractiveness of other countries, heightened by the intensity of media coverage; and the density of migration networks linking individuals and groups in the country of destination with those in the country of origin. Unlike the effects of population growth and the economic crisis, the effects of the other factors will continue to be felt for a long time yet. Without large-scale emigration the countries of the South will have increased difficulties.

Containing illegal immigration and regulating migrant entry impose a high financial and social cost on receiving countries. The problem for individuals is equally great: whether to pay the exorbitant price of illegal immigration or to decide not to improve their situation. Worldwide, greater than ever migration potential is coupled with greater than ever labour movement restrictions. Never before have the interests of the countries of origin and those of the countries of destination been so diametrically opposed. The problem's complexity and the interests of the countries concerned make international cooperation in this field very difficult.

In this type of situation, development assistance is often held up as the magic solution to migration. The reality is quite different, however, because in the short term development will only increase migration potential. It would be hard to imagine development so rapid as to absorb all potential manpower into non-agricultural jobs and offer competitive wages for newly created jobs. At the individual level, which is ultimately the one that counts where migration is concerned, international aid recipients are often not the same people as potential emigrants. The result of all this is well-intentioned rhetoric, but rhetoric that will remain ineffective as long as the macroeconomic requirements for the South's development are not fulfilled. The message of this analysis is relatively straightforward: migration will continue for a long time to come, and it is better to learn to live with it.

There also exist various forms of internal migration, which are not without their problems. In the South, rapid urbanization is swallowing up fertile land, and in the North migration from urban centres is gobbling up energy because of the transport involved. Both these phenomena endanger the maintenance of the agricultural and forest capital necessary for mankind's survival. Jacques Vicari believes that the great North–South disparities in these resources raise questions about the ways of restoring the balance in the development potential of the different regions of the world. In this context, international migration development and greater interdependence in arable land management appear to be reasonable working hypotheses.

The Challenges of Internal Migration
Jacques Vicari

People are on the move in all nations. In the inter- and subtropical regions, they are emigrating from rural to urban areas. 'Irregular settlements'[15] and the number of cities with over ten million inhabitants are on the increase. This puts considerable pressure on fertile land and generates new urban planning problems because of the great needs that have to be met in such a short space of time. In the North the trend is the opposite: the population of the major cities is stationary, or possibly even declining. Because of the discontinuation of low-cost housing construction policies and the place of work–place of residence problem, a large number of people have left the major urban centres and gone to live in distant suburbs or in medium-sized towns. This 'de-urbanization' may accelerate if nothing is done to maintain an acceptable urban environment and halt the spatial separation of employment from the functions of daily living.

The challenge of urbanization has many different facets. Population growth in the subtropical regions means that preparations will have to be made for building within the space of fifty years as many 'regular towns' as were built in the countries of the North over a period of 250 years. During that same fifty-year period the

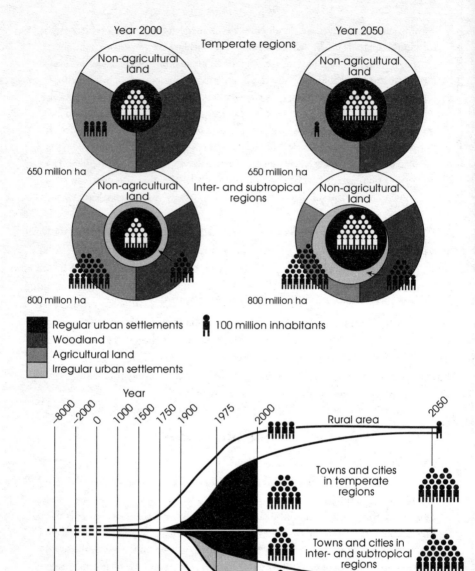

Figure 4.3 *Distribution of Population According to Habitat*

number of 'irregular towns' will be twice as many as at the end of this century. Urbanization policies will have to be based on original solutions, because using the urban planning models and concepts of forty years ago is completely out of the question. Although they enabled city populations to increase from one million to two million inhabitants, they cannot solve the growth problems of an urban centre with a population that will increase from 10 to 20 million inhabitants.

Seen in that light, the Programme of Action's approach and the relevant conceptual tools seem ill-suited to the urbanization actually under way in the countries of the South. This is because they are part of a postwar approach dominated by rebuilding and the creation of 'new towns'. At that time, there was high economic growth and governments funded a large part of social spending, including housing. Although urban-planning inquiries, programmes and projects set up by the industrialized countries' research establishments or by experts trained in the North may help with the planned extension of 'regular towns and cities' to the South, they have no contribution to make to improving 'irregular settlements'. One reason for this is that the scale, speed and mechanisms of this phenomenon are outside the normal framework of reference. The unplanned urbanization of subtropical regions, unlike what happened in the industrialized countries, raises first and foremost the land-use problem, and not the problem of the actual method of urban construction. The problem should therefore be addressed from the point of view of land use.

The total amount of arable and irrigable land is put at 1450 million hectares, 650 million of which are in the temperate regions and 800 million in the tropical regions. The total amount of available fertile land reveals the enormous difference between the countries of the North and those of the South. The situation will become even more dramatic over the next 50 years. This is because between 2000 and 2050 a total of 56 million hectares will be needed in the South for non-agricultural economic activities and for housing the 1.4 billion new inhabitants of 'regular towns'. Moreover, 23 million hectares will be needed for the 2.4 billion inhabitants of 'irregular towns'. At the same time, more than a billion new farmers will need land to cultivate in the rural areas.

There are three scenarios for coping with these projected developments. The first is to do nothing and allow farmers and new urban dwellers to acquire the land they need for survival. The result would be a net reduction in the size of the plots of land available for each peasant family because of increased numbers and growing competition between urban and rural dwellers, similar to the competition between nomadic and settled populations which Biblical civilizations personified in the conflict between the descendants of Cain and Abel.

The second scenario is to open up building land in wooded areas. That, however, would not be feasible unless there were acceptance of large-scale deforestation leading to loss of biodiversity and an appreciable reduction in the amount of oxygen. The third scenario, the most desirable but also the most improbable, is to optimize non-agricultural land use for urban functions so as to leave available agricultural land and forests for other uses. This scenario is unlikely to prevail in urban planning strategies for two reasons. First, the land is often sloping; and secondly, present-day engineers and architects have been trained to find the easiest solutions. Even with a great deal of goodwill, few of them would be able to devise workable solutions for building villages or whole towns on such land.

At this juncture, it is worth extending our analysis to the temperate regions. The slowing of urban growth in those regions, or in some cases even its cessation, gives rise to a twofold problem: maintaining existing towns and cities as an environment for the future; and the decay of the habitat, which means suboptimal use – and even waste and selling off – of agricultural land with great potential. By the end of this century, the industrialized countries' towns and cities will have approximately 1.4 billion inhabitants, with another 300 million by 2050. In the rural areas, there will be at most about a hundred million farmers to work 650 million hectares. In contrast, the 3.3 billion farmers in the South will have to share 800 million hectares. The ratio between the two regions' total populations and their agricultural resources raises several fundamental questions: can the North go so far as to let its land deteriorate or, worse, use it for industrial or residential purposes when it is vital to retain it for providing food for the people of the South?

Moreover, given the magnitude of the existing imbalance, it may be wondered whether the food self-sufficiency ambition of the countries of the South is a realistic one. If it is not, how can development opportunities be harmonized in view of the fact that nature has distributed the means for development so unevenly? Through massive South–North emigration? Through agricultural specialization whereby the vast areas in the North would produce cereal crops, and the small plots of land in the South produce crops appropriate to the climate and the slopes, with North and South exchanging their produce and each country thus able to take what it needs and ensure its food balance?

Whatever solutions are envisaged, consideration must be given to the heat effect of urban activity and 'de-urbanization',[16] which limits in the absolute the quantity of simultaneously usable fossil or nuclear energy. A policy taking account of the population aspect of future developments would therefore be twofold: to safeguard the arable land needed for food production, and the wooded areas needed for breathing; and to ensure that these maintain an acceptable average temperature.

The Political Dimension of Population

The Programme of Action ignores the many political repercussions of the population issue. It does not identify the actual or potential conflicts inherent in current trends and gives the impression that the recommendations cover a politically neutral field. The present situation points to profound changes in the geopolitical balance next century due to population growth and redistribution of demographic potential among the main countries of the world.

According to Jacques Vallin,[17] even if the population growth rate continues to decline, by 2050 there will be approximately 1.3 billion people in today's industrialized countries and 8.5 billion in those countries now referred to as the South, i.e. a ratio of 1 to 7. Just over half of the world population will be Asian, with a growing disparity between East Asia (1.8 billion) and South Asia (3.8 billion). The two superstates – China and India – will still be the most populous countries. India, however, will catch up with China. Population growth will be greatest in Africa, with a threefold increase. The total population of the industrialized countries, on the other hand, will be stationary or will fall slightly. 'In 1950, four European countries (Germany, the United Kingdom, Italy and France) were ranked in the first eleven [in terms of population], each with 40 to 70 million inhabitants... In fifty years' time, they will be only 26th, 27th, 43rd and 30th respectively.'[18]

Urbanization is another aspect of the redistribution of the world's people. In 1950, three cities had ten million inhabitants each – New York and London, the two strongholds of industrial capitalism, and Shanghai. By the end of the century, more than twenty cities will each have over 10 million inhabitants. Statistics here are no longer meaningful in a quantitative sense. Rather, they lead one to consider how sustainable relations may be ensured among peoples in the context of impending upheavals, for behind the variations in numbers, the major changes in the sociocultural pattern of the various populations can already be perceived. The only possible solution for coping with these changes (which are not infallible predictions but credible scenarios) is for there to be the political will to live together under an economic system that enables all societies to be sustainable. Basically, says Jacques Vallin, 'the only real issue is whether we shall be able to accept – in an environment of peace, economic and social development and respect for ecosystems – the geopolitical upheavals to which the diversity of present demographic situations will inevitably lead',[19] for the solution to today's problems is definitely not a demographic one.

The changes on the horizon revive old fears that have never been truly laid to rest. The Cairo Conference – this century's last major international population gathering – passed up the opportunity to play a conciliatory role by making the situation less dramatic and preparing the way for a peaceful change of attitudes within the framework of the new geopolitical balance. The opinion of an intellectual from the South illustrates how necessary dialogue is:

'At a time when the rich have reached the stage of demographic decline, are we not witnessing a gigantic manoeuvre to prevent the emergence of industrial powers that would compete with present-day developed countries? Is there not some hidden fear that three-quarters of the world's population, including Africa's one billion people, will take over everywhere? Or, put another way, how can radical change in North–South ratios within present and future

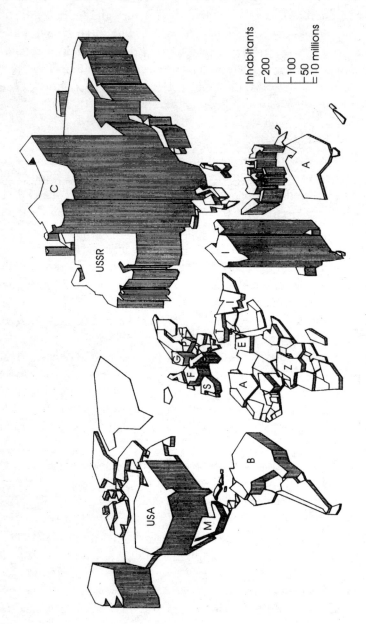

Figure 4.4 *Population by Country in 1950*

Figure 4.5 *Predicted Population by Country for 2050*

demographic imbalances be borne without conflict? That is the crux of the problem.'[20]

Population groups that are now minorities in recently independent states still fear extinction, and large populations continue to feel superior because of their size. Similarly, the aspiration of certain countries to military and commercial superiority persists. Bearing in mind that since 1945 between 13 and 22 million lives have been lost in over 300 conflicts in the countries of the South, there is every justification for wondering what role will be played by demographic change with regard to the power strategies of groups and states throughout the world.

Chapter 5

Practical Measures

The practical measures set out in the Cairo Conference's Programme of Action are more political than technical. This is a new underlying trend in the international negotiations of the 1990s: the technical formulas of socioeconomic development have been replaced by human rights, democracy and partnership with civil society. This approach has been adopted by all United Nations conferences since 1990 in their programmes to combat environmental degradation, child exploitation, poverty or gender inequity. For its part, the Programme of Action recommended the strategies described below.

Programme of Action

Human Rights

Everyone has the right to life, liberty and security of person. Everyone is entitled to all the rights and freedoms set forth in the Universal Declaration of Human Rights without distinction of any kind. Everyone has the right to seek and to enjoy in other countries asylum from persecution. States have responsibilities with respect to refugees as set forth in the Geneva Convention on the Status of Refugees and its 1967 Protocol. Countries must respect individual human rights, paying particular attention to women and the girl child, as well as to migrants, in accordance with the Universal Declaration of Human Rights.

To guarantee those rights, countries are called on to ratify and implement international legal instruments, and to promote, defend and monitor the implementation of individual human rights. The main international legal instruments relevant to the Programme of Action on Population and Development are the Universal Declaration of Human Rights, with particular reference to indigenous people and documented and undocumented migrants; the International Convention on Migrant Workers and Their Families; and the Geneva Convention and the 1967 Protocol on international refugee law, including respect for the principle of *non-refoulement*. Lastly, states are requested to ratify and implement the Convention on the Elimination of All Forms of Discrimination Against Women.

The Programme of Action appeals to governments to strictly enforce marriage law, ensuring that intending spouses are freely consenting and have attained the minimum legal age for marriage, as well as to prohibit sexual mutilation, and prevent infanticide and prenatal sex selection. The human rights enunciated in the Programme include those of victims of all forms of conflicts, ill treatment, violence, exploitation and trafficking in human beings, whether migrants, persons forcibly displaced or young women and children used for pornography or prostitution.

Participatory Democracy

New forms of participation must enable the relevant actors to play a dynamic role in implementing those programmes that concern them. More generally, development programmes must be rooted in the spirit of representative democracy, involving non-governmental organizations and women's associations in particular in policy- and decision-making. These programmes should also enable indigenous people to participate fully in their country's social and political life. To that end, it is necessary to develop democratic institutions, to increase all interested groups' participation in public affairs management and to manage public affairs transparently.

The New Partnership

The partnership between the countries and peoples of the world should be founded upon the acknowledgment of joint responsibility for the planet and each country's responsibility for the others. An effective partnership based on the principles of the Charter of the United Nations should use international cooperation machinery to improve the quality of life of all people. Partners' responsibilities need to be clarified and their efforts better coordinated.

In that context, a number of measures should be encouraged, including technology transfer and the creation of mechanisms to facilitate the collection, analysis and evaluation of demographic information within the framework of networks for exchanging and comparing basic data and experience. This involves increasing the store of knowledge through support for national research and research staff training. Of particular importance is medicine and vaccine production, the idea being to help countries – through technology transfers – to produce generic medicines, vaccines and antibiotics for their domestic market.

Achievement of the Programme's objectives will require the transfer of funds, mainly through official development assistance. The international community is called on to meet, within the framework of its planned financial support, the reproductive health needs of countries with economies in transition (training of personnel, technical assistance and short-term provision of contraceptives). In so doing, it must take care not to reduce assistance to the developing countries. Aid for countries with economies in transition must be additional to that for the poorest countries.

Furthermore, new criteria are needed to ensure that all current funding mechanisms are used to make funds available on conditions that are both preferential and generous, and equitable and sound. In addition, the developing countries could consider enlarging their investment base through the use of funds derived from migrants' savings, pensions and other financial benefits. To that end, the countries of origin could adopt monetary policies, and set in place measures, that would ensure the safety of migrants' financial transfers and help channel savings towards productive investments. Similarly, it is in the best interest of the countries of origin to make full use of the skills acquired by migrants when living abroad.

The Dangers of a Headlong Rush

Ignorance of the Past

A new programme of action inevitably involves a new strategy and means of implementation. Logically speaking, however, the Cairo Programme should have been based on a critical analysis of the achievements of the 1974 World Plan of Action. But unfortunately that was not the case. Although an evaluation was actually prepared,[1] its findings were not integrated into the Programme of Action's recommendations. This gave the impression that a fresh start had been made. Such an impression is all the more regrettable since most people responsible for implementing the 1994 Programme will never have access to the lessons of the past and will lack the information to distinguish between past successes and failures. Although population programmes' main actors are able to create an institutional memory for themselves, this is not true of most of those concerned. Moreover, population issues are often a new area for them. That was the case for most of the non-governmental organizations at the Cairo Conference and for many government representatives who were taking part in international negotiations for the first time. Indeed, many newcomers are now participating in international negotiations.

A comparative approach to the Programme of Action would have been not only essential for guidance purposes but also morally uplifting, because it would have shown that significant progress had been made which deserved to be consolidated and extended. By starting from scratch, the Programme of

97

Action deprived itself of several decades of experience and achievements. In addition, it would have been useful to identify past mistakes: the same causes produce the same effects; and if there is no critical assessment, action is again likely to be misguided.

The Practicability of the New Principles

Reproductive health encompasses and replaces family planning; and democracy and respect for human rights supplant the technical formulas of socioeconomic development. But how is their practicability to be judged? Meeting for the first time after the Conference to discuss the funding of activities, the representatives of the main donor countries appear to have grasped the whole ambiguity of the Programme when they admitted not knowing exactly what the new principles actually meant or how to give effect to them. 'Implementing the Cairo agenda will require both clarifying the concepts involved and testing new approaches in the field'.[2] Put into plain language by Jacques Schwartz, the French Government's representative, this means that in reality 'there is no agreement about what the population programmes encompass or about the percentage of official development assistance to be allocated to the social sectors to which the population programmes belong'.[3]

It is proving to have been a risky strategy to base a substantial part of the Cairo Programme's credibility and contribution on the new concept of 'reproductive health'. Marginalizing the importance of family planning may give the impression that family planning programmes are shameful and that those who once promoted and implemented them are trying suddenly to distance themselves from them. Technically speaking, there is no reason to minimize the beneficial effects of properly designed and executed programmes.

Another new feature of the Programme of Action is the emphasis it places on democracy as 'an instrument for development' and the key role it assigns to non-governmental organizations and the private sector as actors in development. The political framework for action is structured around democratization, decentralization, partnership and increased respect for human rights. Although this was the first time such concepts had been included in a population programme of action, they are not peculiar to population issues, having appeared in virtually the same form in the documents of the other major United Nations conferences held this decade. The strength of this approach lies in the echo effect it creates: the same message repeated from one conference to the next gradually becomes the new basis for international negotiations. As in UN forums, cooperation between Europe and its former colonies is becoming increasingly politicized. For example, the revised text of the Lomé Convention, produced at the end of 1995, recognizes respect for human rights, democracy, the rule of law and good governance as essential factors.[4]

Democracy: a New Fashion or a New Dynamic?

In proclaiming the primordial importance of human rights and democracy, the international community – and particularly the industrialized countries, which are their most ardent champions – imposes upon itself three requirements. The first is to respect those principles.[5] The second is to put them into context by taking account of the situation of countries with political institutions very different from those of Western nations. The third requirement is to spell out the linkages between respect for individual and collective rights, democracy, partnership and the achievement of the population programme's objectives, which seem to be mostly rhetoric at the present time. Moreover, the emphasis on partnership between government and civil society requires clarification of the different actors' roles and responsibilities and, above all, redefinition of their areas of authority.

> *'After thirty years of transfers of capital, technology, managerial models and business cultures, and after the failure of successive remedies, it is now democracy's perilous task to ensure economic development... This perception of democracy as an instrument for the economic development of non-Western societies raises a number of questions: Can actual democratic values and practices be compared with the official ideological view of democracy? Is democracy an unchanging and fully developed category in the West? Is it a universal value or a feature peculiar to a historically and geographically defined sociocultural region? Can it be seen as an instrument for economic development, or is it a specific social balance of power and a specific means of political regulation? Are its fundamental objectives and those of capitalism compatible or diametrically opposed?'[6]*

Those are questions that the main actors in population programmes will not be able to ignore. In her questioning of democracy's universal application, Sophia Mappa raises a fundamental question: how does the development process take root in a particular society's political sphere? In her view, the export of the Western model of democracy to societies built on different standards may lead to a dangerous situation in which 'like structural adjustment, democratic adjustment consolidates the servant–master relationship, rather [than contributing] to the creation of [original] forms of democracy in [non-Western] societies'.[7]

The Multiplicity of Rights

Respect for rights is possible only if they are clearly set out and structured. The different types of rights in the population programme indicate that we have entered a new stage in relations between states and peoples. After recognition of human rights in the eighteenth century and rights to socioeconomic benefits in the nineteenth century, the end of the twentieth century is witnessing the new imperative of group-related *humanitarian* and *collective rights*: the rights of women, children, minorities, migrants, indigenous people, future generations, and so on. 'How can these rights be guaranteed without calling into question the sacrosanct principle of national sovereignty? And how is the transition to be made from the obviously universal nature of individual rights to the intrinsically specific nature of community rights?'[8]

All United Nations programmes are based on the principle of national sovereignty. For example, the population programme affirms the individual's right to freedom of movement but also the right of states to restrict it in the name of national sovereignty. Insofar as states refuse to relinquish their sovereignty for a supranational good, what significance can be attached to international commitments, and how can international negotiations lead to a basis for harmonizing the individual interests of states with those of mankind as a whole? At the present time, ways and means of reconciling national concerns with international interests are still in the early stages of development in many fields, including population.

Population problems pose a question which the concept of national sovereignty cannot by itself answer satisfactorily. That question is as follows: how should the scale of rights and responsibilities be defined, given that reproductive rights could bring about the extinction of the human race, and consumer rights the extinction of the planet? Moreover, in affirming the primacy of individual rights and official and traditional norms, the population programme illustrates the difficulties caused by the principle of juxtaposition (see Chapter 1) currently governing international negotiations. The increased number of rights brings with it the danger of lumping together positive rights (human rights) and the underlying principles of social organization (the right to a healthy and productive life, for example). The eagerness of the international community to proclaim new rights and principles is all the more remarkable since it is frequently loath to take the necessary action to secure respect for the most basic human rights.

In the news

Asian Equations for Human Rights

'Any claim for cultural exceptionalism to exclude human rights is false, non-authentic and is a pretext to justify latent or blatant forms of repression and to legitimise the action which violates the rights of all for the benefit of some individuals,' says the Asian Human Rights Commission charter, drawn up last November.

According to AHRC Executive Director Basil Fernando, indigenous human rights groups are — because of their own experience, knowledge and grass-roots contacts — best positioned to identify the deeper causes of abuses. For example, Westerners often make the assumption that every country has an independent judiciary, which is not the case...

'If someone goes to prison, [Western groups] raise it. But if a particular dam is built and many people suffer, they don't raise it,' said Mr Fernando. 'That's not to say that what they are doing is wrong, but it's limited.'

Jega Ponnambalam of the Asian Students Association said: 'Our position is that human rights issues are partly civil, but also economic. We want an expansion of human rights to include, for example, labour and women's rights.

'In Asia, if you talk about civil and political rights, there have been improvements, especially since 1986. But when you look at economic rights, we have not improved that much.'

John Kohut, South China Morning Post, February 1995, Hong Kong

The New Partnership between Myth and Reality

The Programme of Action assigns an important role to a new category of actors hitherto largely absent from the practical measures of population programmes, one that includes non-governmental organizations, women's groups, members of Parliament and the private sector. A closer examination of the document reveals, however, that the recommendations are so worded that most of the action called for is within the purview of governments. Non-governmental organizations are mainly requested to participate in reproductive health and family planning programmes and advocacy. The private sector is called on to create jobs and provide contraceptives. Members of Parliament are urged to pass the necessary legislation to implement the Programme. Parents are called on to provide their children with financial security and to facilitate adolescents' access to reproductive health services. There is some confusion in the document between those responsible for implementing programmes, the actors involved and the beneficiaries. This may be regarded, however, as indicative of a new, more horizontal approach to partnership, contrasting with the vertical approach hitherto employed.

Since the negotiations in Cairo were between governments, it is hardly surprising that the bulk of the recommendations are addressed to governments, relating either to national responsibilities or to official development assistance. Since the state plays the principal role of the Programme's deviser and main executant, it is difficult to set in motion a genuine partnership synergy in an abstract fashion. However, the wording of the recommendations is broad enough to give room for manoeuvre to the different categories of actors who, within the framework of the specific power relations, will have to negotiate the local and national apportionment of tasks and responsibilities. Insofar as governments are willing, decision-making could be decentralized.

Given the present situation in the North and the South, two questions are worth asking: Are states best placed to take on the tasks assigned them by the Programme of Action? Do they have the political will and the actual means to implement the policies they have undertaken to carry out? The spirit of the recommendations sets great store by the support and responsibility of the welfare state, although its current difficulties appear to have been greatly underestimated. Furthermore, the Programme calls for citizens to be self-supporting within the framework of grass-roots organizations. Such organizations have their technical limitations, however. But more significant is their limited ability to cope with the macroeconomic realities of the market and international relations.

Grass-roots Development

Partnership with local groups is the cornerstone of the new approach to development propounded by Western donor countries. One's first reaction is to welcome this new approach. It is, however, much more demanding than it appears.[9] On the one hand, how can the national representativeness of a non-governmental organization be assessed, and on what grounds can such an organization claim to represent collective interests better than various state bodies? Conversely, implementing a development strategy founded on grass-roots organizations presupposes that they acknowledge the cooperation agencies as valid interlocutors and that the agencies work closely with the local actors, without circumventing or replacing them.

A number of methodological tools are needed to identify the local actors, study their interactions and determine their respective strategies' potentials and limitations. Local government carries out all those functions that help to produce and manage general goods and services. Management encompasses both arbitration and consultation and the development of standards for the orderly integration of individual and collective actions, decisions and choices.

In the news

The Social Actors

Many people are willing to cast aside their privacy if offered a public forum in which to express themselves... In the quest for solutions, there is a very obvious desire that everyone should be able to add a brick to the collective edifice... This mobilization of civil society will become all the more meaningful because it will bring about gradual but tangible changes in order to capitalize on progress, to select and to consolidate. This means discussing analyses and proposals with elected representatives of the people, business leaders, trade unionists, teachers and civil servants without being paralysed by the great divides characteristic of industrial society. It is a matter of drawing up social rules.

We are at a crossroads. Either we are able to give echo to all those voices that ask only to speak out for action, or they are ignored and become discouraged. If the latter happens, people will withdraw into their private lives and the gulf between individuals and institutions will widen, with senseless violence as the only means of expression. Yet precisely because of the new challenges facing it, our democracy can be dynamic once more.

Guy Roustang, Libération, *January 1995, Paris*

The various local government actors do not always work in concert – far from it. This leads to inter-group rivalry and a risk of loss of motivation. As far as the development strategy is concerned, four main groups of local actors are important: the home community (for example, a population occupying a residential area); membership-based communities (for example, voluntary organizations); local government; and state technical services. The second group is increasingly important insofar as it is composed of individuals with the same objectives and values who come together of their own free will for the sole purpose of achieving those objectives.

To make international cooperation as capable as possible of helping groups to carry out development activities in accordance with local priorities, development agencies must consider four questions before deciding on their action strategy:

1. Are the chosen actors bona fide, i.e. acknowledged by the other members of the community?
2. What does the group want to achieve?
3. Is it willing to work with other local actors?
4. What are the group's capacities and what means does it have of realizing its objectives?

'Social demand' is the key development concept, in that it should express the priorities of those people most directly concerned by development. At the present time, either this demand cannot be freely expressed, or it is expressed but not heard because of various administrative, political and sociological obstacles. Case studies have shown that the demand network is often very complex, whereas the supply network is becoming simpler, with aid increasingly going direct to recipients. As a result, intermediate national levels participating in local government in one capacity or another are being marginalized.

Parliamentarians' Responsibility

Members of Parliament nowadays have considerable responsibility for ensuring that governments abide by their international commitments. The Inter-Parliamentary Union, at the international level, and the Council of Europe, at the European level, are the parliamentary bodies most involved in the activities set out in the Cairo Conference's population programme. There are also many *ad hoc* groups.

Since it was established in 1889, the Inter-Parliamentary Union has addressed the population issue on the basis of political concepts wholly similar to those underlying the Programme of Action: respect for individual rights; respect for national sovereignty; and equality among peoples, between the sexes and, more recently, among generations. The regular inclusion of these topics in its conference agenda has helped to inform and shape the political thinking of parliamentarians of all countries on the interrelationships between population factors and the other factors in sociopolitical and economic change. Moreover, the Union has endeavoured to put population issues into perspective within the wider context of peace and international development. From the 1960s onwards, members of Parliament adopted a position of principle whereby an increase in wealth and a more equitable distribution of wealth were two prerequisites for orderly development in which essential resources should be proportional to population growth. In their view, the solution of the population problem required social conditions, political independence and economic progress, creating individual values and social transformations which would lead to propitious demographic change. During that period, and more especially at its 1966 conference, the Union discussed the legitimacy of fertility regulation policies and concluded that when these were implemented by acceptable means, they were as important for development as increased national wealth.

In 1974, the Union endorsed the objectives of the Bucharest World Population Plan of Action. It drew Parliaments' attention to the fact that world population changes would affect the quality of life of all countries, and not merely that of developing countries. In the 1980s, the population issue appeared on the Union's conference agenda every two years, and sometimes more frequently. In most of the development debates during that period speakers referred to the need to integrate population programmes into development activities. The population issue, which had been neglected in the 1970s, made a major comeback during the 1980s at the Mexico City conference and more recently after the Rio conference. As a result, parliamentarians attending international gatherings nowadays discuss population, environmental, economic, social and political issues interdependently.

The work of the Council of Europe, which was established in 1949, is characterized by a commitment to strengthening human rights and pluralistic democracy in the countries of Europe. It organizes discussions, seminars and conferences which provide ideas for its main three bodies: the Committee of Ministers, the decision-making body that signs conventions and agreements; the Parliamentary Assembly, the consultative and deliberative body that draws up resolutions and recommendations; and the Congress of Local and Regional Authorities, which comprises the representatives of the various administrative bodies that are constructing the European entity. Through its various mechanisms the Council seeks solutions to the social problems of the countries of Europe. Population-related matters occupy an important place in its work: migration of workers, protection of national minorities, combating of intolerance, xenophobia and racism, and protection of people in distress, families and individuals. Not content with merely identifying problems, the Council's parliamentarians are endeavouring to develop a political partnership that will help to find effective solutions, both within each country and for Europe as a whole. Since its foundation, the Council has adopted over 150 conventions and treaties. These can be invoked in social action for more rights and greater participation. Of particular importance is the European Social Charter, adopted in 1961, whose objective is to protect twenty-three basic social rights and to encourage the development of social policies more in tune with present-day conditions.

As long ago as 1964 the Council realized the economic and social upheavals that would be caused by population trends in Europe, especially the ageing of the working population and the relative decrease in it. Thereupon it convened a major conference of experts to draw up a research programme and formulate guidelines for a genuine European population policy.[10] The conference's topics and general tone reveal parallels with the set of topics discussed at the Cairo Conference, apart from the religious debate. The main problems identified by the 1964 conference were pregnancy- and childbirth-related mortality; infant mortality, particularly among underprivileged groups; fertility and family planning factors; family formation and status of the family; and the status of women, i.e. education, protection against discrimination, gender equality, and compatibility between working life and family life, with special attention to the most vulnerable women, namely migrant women. Ageing was addressed from the standpoint of its general socioeconomic impact and from that of elderly people's status in relation to their activities. There was a dual approach to migration: improving conditions for migrants' return to their country of origin, and improving living and housing conditions in the receiving country. Another major topic was the urban–rural balance from the standpoint of land-use planning and the impact of migration from rural to urban areas.[11]

The Council of Europe has very often been ahead of its time in grasping the significance of a new phenomenon, and in the nature of the political commitment it has promoted regarding respect for human rights and freedoms, tolerance and pluralism. In population matters, the Council relies for scientific support on the European Population Council and for political support on the Parliamentary Committee on Migration, Refugees and Demography. The purpose of the former is to clarify current trends and draw up scenarios for the future, while the latter's objective is to find the best means of translating these trends into concerted political action at the level of the Council's thirty-three member countries.

Generally speaking, informed and effective parliamentary action is founded upon reliable information about the national demographic situation (and the demographic situation of other countries) and about the medium- and short-term implications of population trends, and upon a framework for assessing the impacts of the options from among which a government must choose. This framework, which is inevitably based on judgments about standards, i.e. on a particular model of society, should be made as explicit and transparent as possible (a political purpose), in the knowledge that each option has positive and negative impacts of varying scope and intensity. It is necessary therefore to identify those who will have to bear the cost of policies (a specific social group, young people or future generations, for instance) and create the appropriate palliative mechanisms. Legislation is required in order to provide individuals with social and financial security, and take account of their diversity and changing needs. Lastly, tasks must be reapportioned among political leaders and economic-decision makers so that the latter are more involved in support for social reproduction and no longer merely concerned with the output of material goods. At the present time, only the first of these conditions is anywhere near fulfilment.

International Cooperation

The Programme of Action assigns an important role to international cooperation at the financial level and at the level of technology transfer and exchange of information and experience. Like the system of international relations and the institutions governing them, international cooperation is going through a turbulent period. Reform to harmonize its procedures with partnership's new principles is proving difficult because of the burden of its politico-technocratic past. Despite declarations of openness with regard to civil society, official development assistance remains a state matter, since cooperation budgets are approved within a framework that does not generally include national non-governmental organizations. Only five countries – Norway, Denmark, Sweden, the Netherlands and Finland – have reached the target of 0.7 per cent of Gross National Product (GNP) allocated to international development. There is a very good chance, however, that Finland will fall short of that target in the near future, as it has substantially cut its aid. By contrast, the average level of OECD countries' aid was 0.37 per cent in 1992 and 0.29 per cent in 1993.

Contrary to predictions, it has not proved possible to use the post-Cold War peace dividend for the benefit of international development. The number of ethnic and nationalistic conflicts has soared astronomically and a growing proportion of aid is now allocated for refugees, displaced populations and other emergency situations requiring rapid, effective and large-scale responses. The 'new international political disorder'[12] is accompanied by an increase in humanitarian aid, thus disadvantaging development programmes. International aid currently totals about $55 billion, i.e. half of the agreed amount for funding the Agenda 21 programme which the UN member states approved by consensus at the Rio Conference.[13]

With export industry promotion and direct linkage between political support and aid increasing, most aid money is used first to further donor countries' interests. The majority of donor countries (between 65 and 90 per cent) tie aid to the purchase of goods and services in the donor country. Economic difficulties in the industrialized countries merely exacerbate the situation by putting increased pressure on development aid agencies to derive the maximum benefit from aid. In addition, 'security needs' (i.e. what countries consider to be a strategic interest in a particular part of the world) still play an important role in aid's geographical distribution, which in this case is often coupled with significant military aid.

New needs have arisen because of the political changes in Eastern Europe. Consequently, part of the aid once provided to the poorest nations has been reallocated to that region. As far as sectoral priorities are concerned, numer-

Help! Too Much Aid!

The village of Masinandraina is set in the midst of a bucolic landscape to the south of Tananarive, three hours away by road... Its 600 inhabitants are used to seeing visitors arrive from far away. 'All the NGOs of Madagascar have come to sound us out ... all the international organizations have sent representatives: the World Bank, the ILO, the African Development Bank, etc. Even seminars are held here'... In this small village, five development agencies are vying for the opportunity to extend credit on the most advantageous terms...

Masinandraina is not the only place where the peasants of Madagascar have more benefactors than they know what to do with. In the Antsirabe region, about a hundred local or foreign NGOs, state organizations and groups of missionaries have set up shop. Some of them want to help the peasants with their work; others want to improve a particular crop or combat poverty. Among all these well-intentioned people, the peasants feel rather lost. In a particular village ... the state organization encourages rice growers to use chemical fertilizers, whereas a local NGO strongly advises against it. Missionaries donate materials to the villagers and pay for the labour needed to build dykes, while others demand that the peasants build them themselves... 'There's too much aid and too many people are involved. The duration of projects is too short. Most of them don't last more than five years. Donors need to agree among themselves.' Despite his efforts, Tiana Ralison has been unable to persuade the NGOs to harmonize their approach to rural development. Each NGO thinks it has the right formula.

According to Mr Ralison, lack of coordination causes a great deal of waste. At best, half of the aid reaches the people it is intended for. The rest fuels the development machine, which has become one of the region's biggest employers. [Despite] its formidable potential ... 'the region is still in an advanced state of decline owing to mismanagement of aid and funding, and to the short-lived nature of the aid projects'. Despite the abundance of aid, the peasants live precariously. The question today, however, is who needs aid more – the peasants or the NGOs.

Nzekoué Libéré, Syphia, July 1994, Dakar

ous forums have underlined the importance of devoting at least 20 per cent of funds to human development (education, health, improved status of women, family planning, etc.). However, the countries represented at the Social Summit in Copenhagen refused to endorse that approach, wording the relevant recommendation in such a way as to give themselves all the necessary latitude for allocating their aid as before. In 1988–89, none of the 15 major donor countries devoted 20 per cent of its aid to human development activities.

Figures and trends indicate that we are entering a period of reduced development aid. But beyond that, the pattern of international aid appears confused. In terms of what they say, all countries seem to have the same priorities: combating poverty, strengthening the foundations of human rights and democracy, combating environmental degradation and improving the status of women. In the implementation of these priorities, however, matters are complicated by cumbersome bureaucracy, complex decision-making machinery and multiple sources and means of funding. These factors impose upon aid recipients constraints that are incommensurate with the positive advantages they will ever be able to hope to derive from the aid received. This is in keeping with the principle that 'an assisted economy quickly transforms a bureaucracy into a superfluous staff and organizations industry'.[14]

In the news

Cultural Gulf the Cause of US–China Friction

When the United States set February 4 as the deadline for China to comply with its demands on copyright protection, both countries already knew it was one deadline that would not be met... The seat of government was at a virtual standstill because of the Lunar New Year holidays, still one of the most widely-celebrated festivals in China... Yet the US announced promptly on February 4 that it would impose sanctions on US$1.08 billion worth of Chinese goods if no agreement were reached by February 26...

[T]he US–China trade friction is another manifestation of the cultural chasm between the West and Asia ... that has led to misunderstanding and mistrust... On the part of the US: The Americans demonstrated cultural insensitivity by fixing a deadline that coincided with the Lunar New Year, a period highly auspicious to the Chinese... On the part of China: ... They do not comprehend fully the deep, almost religious respect and high regard which Americans have for the creative technical process responsible for sending the first man to the moon and many of the world's technological marvels...

China has also underrated the tremendous domestic clout of the US motion picture and music industries... Hollywood movies and the musical talent of American performers have done far more to promote US influence than any other product with the 'Made-in-USA' stamp...

Certainly, stronger cultural ties are crucial to improving relationships and erasing misunderstandings between the world's big economic and political players.

Felix Soh, The Straits Times, *February 1995, Singapore*

The population programme states that international aid should total $5.7 billion in the year 2000 and $7.2 billion in 2015, not counting the resources the countries of the South will be able to mobilize. Given present aid trends, however, such amounts are unlikely to be actually released. In the case of the population programme as in that of the Rio environment programme, the proposed sums remain academic hypotheses. Moreover, like Jean Chesneaux, we may ask 'whether the North can keep to its benchmarks such as aid, cooperation and solidarity with the South while endeavouring at the same time to preserve the benefits accruing from its history'.[15] Apart from money, what seems to be lacking most in international relations is a genuine climate of dialogue and mutual respect. Profound ignorance about other people, superficial contacts and swift rotation of international 'experts' help to maintain the gulf between individuals and peoples, who nevertheless face the same challenges.

Chapter 6
Review of the International Negotiations

Different Assessments

Assessments of the Cairo Conference's Programme of Action vary considerably. Essentially, there are two very different interpretations. According to the first of these, which is the dominant one in terms of visibility and impact on the main donor countries, the negotiations 'succeeded in transcending macro-demographic objectives to arrive at an integrated population and development strategy centred on individual well-being and the emancipation of women'.[1] According to the second one, which is much less structured and institutionalized, the Programme of Action neglected the macroeconomic problems and fundamental sociopolitical challenges underlying the demographic situation. These two interpretations are not only common among experts, but interestingly enough are also found in the media in identical form. On the whole, the media in the English-speaking countries endorse the first one, and those in other countries the second. For example, *The Times* of London welcomed the Conference's many recommendations for improving the status of women, whereas *Le Soir* of Brussels expressed complete disillusionment, and deplored the lack of substantive discussion about the linkage between our demographic future and the future *per se*.

The Times

Despite strong reservations from the Vatican and several leading Muslim countries, the population conference in Cairo ended yesterday with more agreement on urgent steps to educate women, improve access to family planning and stabilise the world's burgeoning population than any of the 182 delegates had thought possible at the start... The United Nations-sponsored conference gave broad approval to a 20-year programme of action intended to emphasise individual choice in family planning, improve the status, health and rights of women, bolster development in Third World countries and raise a greater proportion of funds for population policies from developed nations.

Michael Binyon, The Times, September 1994, London

Le Soir

Perhaps it was not to be expected that the mountain that would give birth to anything other than a mouse... Fifteen thousand delegates took leave of each other yesterday in Egypt, having vaguely promised ... to do nothing... Whole paragraphs [in the Programme of Action] are masterpieces of gobbledegook. There was not a single specific promise ... nor was there a figure or commitment somewhere in among the insipid phraseology dictated by the industrialized countries' overcautious reflexes regarding development aid or the right of asylum... No sooner had the conference started than it got bogged down. And it was not the weary NGOs that helped to bring it back to life. However much they all hang together and however powerful they are when it comes to environmental lobbying, they are as different from one another as Simone de Beauvoir was from Mother Teresa where the emancipation of women is concerned... This failure would not have been so bad if the Cairo exercise had been merely an exercise in style. But is any subject more fundamental to the world than its own future?

Joëlle Meskens, Le Soir, September 1994, Brussels

Three major issues occupied the attention of French, Belgian and German newspapers during the negotiating process.[2] Before the Conference, journalists focused exclusively on the alliance taking shape between the Vatican and the Islamic nations. During the Conference they concentrated on abortion, which was at the centre of the dispute that was raging. They did so to such an

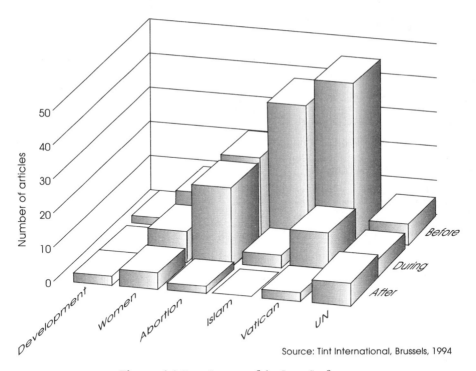

Source: Tint International, Brussels, 1994

Figure 6.1 *Press Coverage of the Cairo Conference*

extent that the general public may have had the impression that the
Conference was all about abortion. After the Programme of Action had been
adopted, those journalists who had not lost interest by then deplored the
Conference's exceedingly superficial treatment of its main theme – development. A number of newspapers had predicted that the Conference would
become increasingly obsessed with abortion. Many editorial writers saw this
as a sign that the industrialized countries preferred to let the Conference
become bogged down in a matter which was of secondary interest compared
with world population problems. This meant that it would not touch on more
sensitive issues such as official development assistance funding and the dispute
surrounding the industrialized nations' economic production and consumption patterns. Journalists also noted that migration proved to be of little
interest and that its economic, political and cultural aspects had been largely
glossed over. Some journalists thought that the Conference had been a diplomatic power play where consensus had taken precedence over the substance
of the international community's commitment. Avoiding extremes, the French
newspaper *Le Monde* offered a lucid but purportedly optimistic assessment of
the Conference.

┌─ *In the news* ───┐

Le Monde

Although a somewhat mixed assessment may be made of the conference on women and the family, it has to be said that there was widespread disappointment as regards everything development-related. Other than recognizing a non-binding 'right to development', the Conference said nothing at all about development. Nevertheless, there is a gradually emerging hope that the major donor countries' aid will be directed towards a more global approach to demographic policies and a less simplified view of population trends.

Alexandre Buccianti and Guy Herzlich, Le Monde, September 1994, Paris

└───┘

Different Outlooks

It is hardly surprising that *The Times* on the one hand and *Le Soir* and *Le Monde* on the other interpreted the Cairo Conference differently: their interpretations reflect the intellectual positions peculiar to two different worlds that have never been on the same wavelength as far as population issues are concerned. Indeed, since the 1950s there have been two main approaches in the international population debate: the Anglo-Saxon one, dominated by the Americans; and the Latin one, of which the French are probably the most typical representatives. Broadly speaking, the Anglo-Saxon position is Malthusian and favours fertility reduction, whereas the Latin position is in favour of a rising birth rate and population growth. 'In the US population research dynamics and funding have been bound up with concern about population growth, particularly in the Third World, and the establishment of the "family planning business" in the countries of that region. In France, on the other hand, the impetus for population research derives from national demographic concerns, particularly the low birth rate.'[3] In international negotiations it is the Anglo-Saxon approach that prevails. The movement embodying it is firmly established politically, institutionally and scientifically. Its counterpart, on the other hand, has concentrated largely on national population trends and has not sought to justify itself to the outside world. As a result, international debate since the 1950s has been quite naturally structured around the set of problems defined by the English-speaking world.

The Latin Approach

In both France and Italy, population research has tended to concentrate heavily on national problems, and there has been only a very limited interest in (or even intellectual openness to) international problems. Fortunately, this tendency has decreased in recent years, and high-quality experts are emerging from newly established research centres.

In the case of France, these developments can be explained by the political objectives of French demography and by society's demographic features. In 1946, Alfred Sauvy described France's situation in the following terms: 'The consequences of the quantitative and qualitative decline in the population of France are now being painfully felt. The country today is bearing particularly heavy burdens – quite apart from those of the two world wars – at a time when it is anxious to ensure its security and the cohesion of its empire, help its old people and maintain its role in modern civilization'.[4] Because fertility had declined earlier in France than anywhere else (in the first half of the eighteenth century),

> *'the inadequate overall birth rate was portrayed as a very serious problem for France as a nation and a State... During the same period, influential English intellectuals stressed the importance of the human race's quality from a eugenic viewpoint and deplored the excessive fertility of the poor, who were alleged to be hereditarily less intelligent than the rest of the population. These two almost diametrically opposed outlooks explain why views on population in France and England have been different.'[5]*

The Anglo-Saxon Approach

Three factors have helped to make the Anglo-Saxon approach the dominant one in international negotiations since the Second World War: an official set of ideas based on the threat of a so-called world population crisis; generously funded scientific research into the fertility of the countries of the South; and a strong presence on the international scene due to considerable policy-making ability and intense lobbying.

The Population Threat

A population policy is always a state policy, whether it is for domestic or overseas use. The US, the self-proclaimed guardian of world order, saw the rapid population growth in the countries of the South as a threat. By propagating the notion of a 'world population crisis' it developed a line of thought to justify its ideas. According to Samuel Preston, the threat perceived explains why population research in the US expanded in order to support policy-making and was funded in particular by the National Institutes of Health, to

2

the tune of tens of millions of dollars a year, to study the fertility of the countries of the South. Government policy was along the same lines. 'AID [the Agency for International Development] has identified family planning programs ... as the proper means of reducing the level of fertility in a population. The rationale for this supply-side focus is that it expands rather than restricts the domain of personal choice in reproduction and that governments have no business attempting to alter an individual's childbearing preferences'.[6]

The Framework Concept of Demographic Transition

The concept of demographic transition has played an important part in the development of the Anglo-Saxon approach. Unlike other concepts, it has seen the light of day twice. It was first enunciated in 1929 by Warren S. Thompson, but aroused no interest. It surfaced again in 1945 in the work of Frank W. Notestein and embarked on a brilliant career within the framework of American reconstruction policy as applied to underindustrialized countries.[7] In the immediate postwar period the US was seeking a conceptual framework and data that would enable its economic planners and foreign relations experts to reorganize the world market and structure political relations from the standpoint of American interests. The concept of demographic transition and the closely related one of modernization formed an extremely useful conceptual framework. Initially, there were two radically different versions of the transition theory. The first of these, propounded by Notestein between 1945 and 1949, held that mortality and fertility reductions occur after a long process of modernization involving economic, sociocultural and political changes. At the end of the 1940s, however, Notestein and his team did a conceptual about-turn and stated the opposite – namely, that the fertility level was not to be regarded as resulting from a set of socioeconomic factors, but rather as something that could be changed independently of the wider social context. This second version of the transition theory opened the way to justifying policies and programmes for fertility level reduction. These were based on the argument that fertility reduction would bring about socioeconomic and cultural changes.

What is important here is not so much the substance of the theory as the political reasons for its development and form. The period between 1945 and 1950 was marked by America's concern for its security and by the deployment of a strategy to combat communism. Population policies were much favoured by the US. According to Simon Szreter, the initial purpose of American fertility control policies was to provide an alternative to the structural changes advocated by the communist approach to development. 'Policymakers and conservative public opinion in the West, anxious to preserve and promote liberal values, were extremely wary of any involvement with wider-ranging social and economic policies seeking structural changes possibly with redistributive implications. Provision of family planning for voluntary acceptance therefore appealed as a safe liberal policy for development.'[8] However, since actual facts proved more various and complex than could be deduced from the transition model, it was modified to recognize all possible types of causality between socioeconomic, cultural and demographic factors.

Policy-making Between Science and Ideology

Between the population issue's sudden entry into the political debate and the Cairo Conference, various explanations of population and development linkages held centre stage one after another. For the purposes of elucidation, these may be divided into three main groups which attached particular importance to physical, human and environmental capital respectively.[9] Nowadays many different factors are used in the analysis process as part of a variable-geometry syncretism whereby everyone derives from different models the arguments that best meet their current needs.

The end of the Second World War marked the beginning of a high-growth period which led to an increase in the standard of living in the West. It was a period of rapid industrial development sustained as necessary by considerable financial aid offsetting a lack of capital (Marshall Plan, official development assistance). Trade grew, resulting in increasingly close integration of international economic relations. With several notable exceptions, most economists believed that the engine for growth was the formation of physical capital, and that savings and investment were the main development factors. This view was the foundation of the Western industrialized countries' position at the Bucharest Conference. These countries argued that high population growth hindered development because it reduced the savings rate and the state's investment potential. Their assessment of the population situation both defined the issue involved and set out the solution. Rapid population growth, they said, stemmed from women's and couples' inability to have the desired number of children. To reduce the fertility rate, it was therefore sufficient to meet the 'unmet demands for family planning'. In their view, this solution benefited both women and society.

Development theory in the 1980s was dominated by a new proposition: the formation of human capital is the driving force in economic growth. The development policies applied to the countries of the South now stressed agriculture, rural development and the informal economy. According to

Jean-Claude Chasteland, the World Bank report presented at the time of the Mexico City Conference is an excellent illustration of this change of perspective. 'In its report the World Bank argues for population growth reduction on the basis of the observation that in Third World countries with rapidly growing populations such growth hinders education and health programme development, and therefore human resource development. This "simplified Malthusianism" brings the debate about population growth impact onto new ground. In addition, the debate is now part of the new concern with the human aspects of development.'[10]

Towards the end of the 1970s and the beginning of the 1980s, environmental degradation assumed greater importance in population discussions and the concept of 'carrying capacity' gradually became the criterion for sustainable development. Population growth was increasingly singled out as a major cause of environmental degradation. The argument was twofold: large, poor families destroy their environment to survive (erosion and deforestation), and rapid population growth compels countries to sacrifice their natural resources in order to obtain foreign exchange. This is required for building infrastructures and funding the social services needed to improve the population's standard of living. From that perspective, concern began to be expressed about the populations of ecologically vulnerable areas (arid regions, mountain and coastal areas) and displaced populations living in hazardous economic and environmental conditions (refugees, victims of natural disasters, etc.).

Nowadays, the sole point of policy-making with respect to the countries of the South is to assert the negative nature of population growth. For that purpose, a number of disparate arguments are taken from a collection of basically relevant analyses. It is scarcely possible, however, to draw the required conclusion from these analyses. This leads to an inconsistency between the list of arguments and the positions to which they give rise, as illustrated by two examples – a document to guide Australian development assistance policy,[11] and an analysis by the US National Academy of Sciences[12] – both summarized in Table 6.1 below.

More than ever before, the portrayal of population–development relationships draws more on ideology than on scientific observation. A new approach evolved between the 1980s and the Cairo Conference, one that borrows its arguments simultaneously from several theories. The most common version links together poverty, population growth, environmental degradation, women's inferior status and low level of education, and high maternal and infant mortality. The treatment of these issues depends on events and the aims of the relevant interest groups. Consequently, the reasoning appears fragmented and uncertain, capable of being endlessly reconstructed.

Table 6.1 *Inconsistencies in Policy-making*

Analysis	Conclusion
Poverty: there is little direct evidence on whether rapid population growth causes poverty. *Environment:* population growth impacts are not wholly positive or negative; they depend on the flexibility of individuals' and groups' reaction to increased population pressure. *Family size:* it can affect a child's long-term nutritional status, but the effect is moderated by family structure and culture. *Education:* the number of children in a family has a relatively minor impact on their education. *Population growth:* growth may have negative or positive effects; neither the net impact nor its magnitude can be determined on the basis of existing observations and knowledge.	Population growth reduction benefits health, economic development, housing, food availability, poverty reduction, environmental protection and perhaps also education.
Analysis	Conclusion
Population growth impact is difficult to quantify because of the complexity and multiplicity of the relationships involved and the diversity of local situations. Because of varied response and substitution possibilities, population growth impact on economic development is probably slight.	Rapid population growth impacts negatively on the development of most developing countries.

No doubt because of the problems' fluctuating nature, no delegation in Cairo sought to defend one theory in preference to another. That the arguments are vague and variable is due to a large extent to the multiplicity of the viewpoints supported by various sources of information and discussion.

Several lessons may be drawn from the differing approaches to the population issue. The virtue of the Anglo-Saxon approach is that it has drawn the international community's attention to a number of very real problems by promoting high-quality research that has served as a basis for valuable family planning programmes. Its weakness is that it considers only one option for

The Misunderstanding

The climate change debate is a good example of the links that have developed between science and politics in the last ten years... From the hole in the ozone layer to the greenhouse effect, via the loss of biodiversity, it is the scientists who have sounded the alarm... Unfortunately, however, politics all too often prefers dogmas to nuances. To make matters worse, in our media-ridden age, it is simple ideas that command the ratings and the opinion polls... From one end of the ecological-political scene to the other, people refer to ratings and polls − either to call for radical action straight-away, with no regard for its potentially adverse economic impact, or to reject action on the ground that 'we are not sure about anything'...

It is as if some people are intent on viewing science as a replacement for ideolo-gies that have collapsed... 'There is a complete misunderstanding... Decision-makers ask us for magic formulas, but all we can give them is knowledge'... Any corrective action in these areas inevitably has positive and negative consequences. This is where the basic role of politics − to arbitrate − comes in.

Jean-Paul Dufour, Le Monde, *March 1995, Paris*

meeting population challenges: fertility reduction in the South. Conversely, the development of the Latin approach has been marked by greater ideologi-cal independence as regards population's international dimension. This approach, however, lacks the practical basis and international visibility that are needed for it to become a force to be reckoned with in the debate. Consequently, approaching world population problems from a single view-point makes it more difficult to achieve a sense of collective responsibility. If problems are to be understood and a fruitful dialogue pursued, both thought and action have to be pluralistic. Seen from this angle, the controversy fuelled by the Catholic Church and the Islamic authorities had the virtue of introduc-ing into the debate a number of dimensions which, although neglected, were vital in negotiations on issues of life and death, sexuality and the purposes of the family. Through their emphasis on these dimensions − ethical and cultural − the Churches kept alive an issue for which a single-reference model could not provide a definitive response. Unfortunately, however, since the only solu-tion they offered was acceptance of their own dogmas, they were unable to get a productive debate under way.

Population research and negotiations need to be given fresh impetus for two reasons. The first is a practical one. Governments' ability to implement the Programme of Action depends on their understanding of the problems and

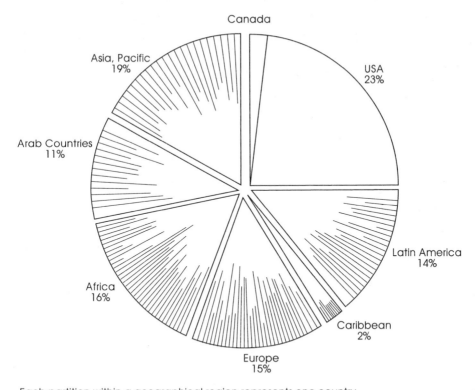

Each partition within a geographical region represents one country

Source: UN, *Report on the Cairo Conference*, 1995

Figure 6.2 *Distribution of Non-Governmental Organizations at the Cairo Conference According to their Region of Origin*

their capacity for formulating coherent options. There are five major inconsistencies in the Programme. If these are not properly identified and resolved, they will prevent the international community from giving effect to its recommendations. The second reason is conceptual, and relates to the very future of demography and its usefulness in clarifying local and worldwide challenges. The Anglo-Saxon approach to population has deadlocked the debate by making the demographic perspective irrelevant. Because its scope is restricted to reproduction's microsocial dimension, it is incapable of shedding the light needed to define current world challenges and is therefore incapable of setting out the appropriate solutions for coping with current population trends.

Resolving the Inconsistencies

The inconsistencies described below did not all emerge from the most recent

121

population negotiations – far from it. Some of them are to be found in the Bucharest world plan, while others crystallized at the Cairo Conference.

Individual, Family and State: Are Their Rights Compatible?

Like the 1974 Bucharest plan, the Cairo Programme of Action refers to three different entities: the individual, the family and the state, each with its own rights and privileges. The difficulty here is that in reality the rights of each are often incompatible. Two examples will illustrate this. First, the individual's right to freedom of movement exists alongside the state's right to regulate that freedom in accordance with its own interests. Second, there is a conflict between individual rights and those of the family. For example, the Programme of Action asserts adolescents' right to confidentiality and to avail themselves of reproductive health and contraceptive services. However, although it fully endorses self-reliance, it also stresses the 'duty' of parents to guide adolescents in this area.

To resolve these inconsistencies or dilemmas, depending on whether a more or less normative approach is adopted, there will be a temptation to put forward different methods of negotiating rights and duties. As far as international migration is concerned, there has been an apparent failure to establish a basis for discussion to reconcile states' interests with those of individuals. With regard to adolescents, some countries invoke young people's ability to make judgments rather than invoking the juridical concept of legal majority. That is a flexible approach for coping with young people's sexual behaviour. Depending on a country's social structure and its cultural standards, recognition of the ability to make judgments may be embodied in an amendment to existing law (which some European countries are planning) or may be achieved through social tolerance and acceptance of realities.

Cultural Specificity Versus the Predominance of the Western Model

The second type of inconsistency in the Programme of Action is the discrepancy between the stated need to take account of each country's cultural specificity and the strength of a reference model that sets not only the objectives to be achieved but also *the manner in which* they are to be achieved. Although it acknowledges the diversity of values and social structures, the Programme is strongly marked by the pre-eminence of Western industrial nations' concepts, values and standards for society's functioning. This is illustrated by the emphasis on the individual instead of his or her support network;

women's paid employment as the criterion for self-reliance and social status; family responsibility categorized as spouses' responsibility; the sharing of domestic tasks between husband and wife; the importance of sexual satisfaction; and the state's role in protecting individuals. Given its diverse forms and purposes, the concept of the family raises questions about the relationships between the family, the state and the individual, which vary from one region to another. In some regions and cultural traditions, for example among most so-called indigenous people, the group takes precedence over the individual. Catholicism and Islam, on the other hand, give precedence to the family over its members.

The Programme of Action's implicit assertion that individual self-fulfilment – particularly sexual self-fulfilment – takes precedence over respect for society's rules caused considerable disagreement. Depending on the country, there are a number of reasons why a woman may seek or spurn sexual relations; and the Western values of self-reliance and self-fulfilment here are not necessarily those of all women as individuals, or of all cultures as communities. Moreover, the model of relations between spouses within the family is a paradigm which is itself contradicted by the Programme's recognition of the family's polymorphous nature and the different forms it takes according to the social, cultural and political systems prevailing. Since the bulk of the recommendations are addressed to the countries of the South and the reference model is identified with the societies of the North, there is inevitably a feeling of unreality. Finally, the proposed solutions often seem too standardized to take account of the diversity of situations; social groups in both the North and the South are mixed and their attitudes vary. The proposed ways of improving individual quality of life bear the mark of a social model that has evolved in the West. According to Joel Jakubec, this model has more in common with the 'Protestant reflex' than with a religious dogma.

The Protestant Reflex
Joel Jakubec

In-depth study of the Programme of Action on Population and Development and attempts to understand the ethical and philosophical reasons for its conclusions reveal that it has a particular vision of mankind which governments have comprehensively endorsed despite a number of reservations. This vision is closely related to the 'Protestant universe', which bears the last traces of the Reformation in the sixteenth century, which was itself the result of a wide-ranging network of influences.

Although populations living in the same place differ greatly nowadays, mainly Protestant regions still share a number of reflexes: a concern for self-reliance and commitment; a desire to make free use of all available material, intellectual and

123

scientific resources; and a distrust of hierarchies of any sort, which are suspected of encroaching on individual rights. This is given expression in an approach to the individual that emphasizes his actions and ability, not his ancestry or inherited privileges. The word 'reflex' is used here advisedly, because in the last years of this century, when knowledge of the Bible has been almost completely overshadowed, what we have now is more a pragmatic attitude to life than the expression of a doctrine or a firm belief, and even less the affirmation of a dogma. Protestants feel very free, sometimes unrestrainedly so, regarding issues such as euthanasia, genetic research, contraception and abortion. On the other hand, they freely accept other people's choices even when different from their own. Lastly, they aspire to a certain quality of life based on material comfort combined with freedom of enterprise, which is the foundation of the ideology of strongly individualistic development.

These behaviours with regard to choices about life and society are the visible consequences of events upon which Protestant thought is based, but of which most people are not aware. Three axioms, mostly developed in the sixteenth century and based on Old and New Testament scriptural exegesis, explain largely how those behaviours came about. The first is political. Referring to the election of David in the Second Book of Samuel – 'All the elders of Israel elected David king in the presence of Jehovah' – the reformer Théodore de Bèze (1519–1605) says: 'There was a solemn oath whereby the King and the People submitted themselves to God – that is, to the observance of His laws, both ecclesiastical and political; then there was another mutual oath between the King and the People'. Commenting on this passage, Ivo Rens says that 'as a result, the people possess rights in their own name, and the magistrates or the States General are empowered to uphold them even against the king if he were to become a tyrant'.[13] Through the intermediary of Marnix de Sainte-Aldegonde, a disciple of Calvin and Bèze, this statement of the people's rights was to influence the Declaration of Independence of the United Provinces (the Netherlands) in 1587. A similar statement is to be found in the People's Covenant laid before the Parliament of England in 1648, and in the American Declaration of Independence of 1776. According to the historian Geisendorf, the foundation of modern public law is directly inspired by the Reformation.[14] Protestantism has had a great influence on the development of law (individual rights and national sovereignty) and the international spirit. For example, President Woodrow Wilson chose Geneva as the headquarters of the League of Nations because it was, as he said, 'Calvin's city'.

The second axiom concerns the attitude towards science. Marvelling at the Creation and Man's genius for invention in his meditation on the Book of Job, Calvin asks: 'Where do all the sciences come from? Are they not so many streams that flow from the fountain of the Spirit of God? Let us learn not to scorn God's blessings when they manifest themselves in men, but to profit from them and turn them to our own use'.[15] The reformers were therefore mindful of scientific progress and of the benefits that humankind could derive from it. This may be seen as one of the reasons for the advancement of biomedical research and especially the development of modern contraceptive methods, without any moral impediments arising.

The reformers were also mindful of education and educational matters. Particular attention was given to language – the main means of acquiring and spreading, first Biblical and then secular knowledge. 'The Reformation thrust the teacher to the forefront everywhere. It taught people to read and write. It wanted education for everyone. Consequently, by the end of the seventeenth century northern Europe was more educated than southern Europe, whereas the opposite had been true in the Middle Ages'.[16] Two centuries later, development and gender equity are a central factor in most of the international community's programmes of action.

The third axiom is social justice, a subject particularly studied during the Reformation. Noting that human labour is one of God's requirements, Calvin concludes: 'As for craftsmen and tradesmen, we know that their entire income derives from their ability to earn their living, for they have no income from meadows and fields. So, since God has thus placed their lives in their own hands, namely their toil, when they are deprived of necessities, it is as if their throats had been cut'.[17] This approach to the link between work and social justice – work being regarded not only as a duty but also a right – is today at the heart of the debate on the fundamental principles of social justice and the choice between retributive and distributive justice.

The brief historical outline above is not intended to provide a key for interpreting the whole of the Programme of Action on Population and Development. It is merely an attempt to throw light on a multifaceted social model that echoes the importance attached by Protestant thought to the concepts of individual self-reliance, economic development, education and social justice.

Interrelated Problems but Separate Responsibility

There is a third inconsistency in the Programme of Action – between the interdependent approach to problems and the dualistic approach to solutions. The Programme of Action is based on the assumption that population growth, production and consumption patterns, environmental degradation and poverty are interrelated. However, where solutions are concerned the issue is split in two: it is said on the one hand that the countries of the South have various population problems, and on the other hand that the countries of the North have a duty to alter their production and consumption patterns. Although the tasks of the countries of the South are spelt out (establishment of reproductive health and family planning programmes, and improvement of women's status), the Programme of Action does not specify the precise implications of the industrialized countries' responsibilities. By splitting up responsibilities and stressing only those of the South, the Programme of Action deprives population issues of their global implications, international negotiations of their universality and responsibility of its collective nature.

The Integration of Population and Development: the End of a Myth

The Anglo-Saxon approach welcomes the fact that there is at last a genuine integrated population and development strategy. However, as any reasonably perceptive person knows, such a strategy has never existed other than as a collection of words. After three decades of political talk about the need to integrate population into development, and after the establishment of numerous 'population units' in the countries of the South to translate the links between population and development into reality, the results are very disappointing. Even the United Nations Population Fund, which funded many such projects, does not believe that there has been much success in constructing models that explain this twofold dynamic.[18] Not only has no theory demonstrated linkages between population and development, but also facts tend to indicate that developments increasingly do not conform to the standard model: demographic transition–industrial development–population balance.

Demographic transitions vary in terms of their magnitude, duration and modes, and occur within the context of other transitions – epidemiological, educational, democratic, economic and energy-based. Although population dynamics depend partly on global interactions, the forms and directions they take locally are extraordinarily varied and testify to the different development rates in the various parts of the world. Compared with this movement, the notion of ideal, optimal or balanced population seems devoid of meaning, since it may be said, as Michel Loriaux says, that 'there is no such thing as an ideal population *per se*; a population can be declared good or bad only in relation to clearly defined societal objectives'.[19] Moreover, to address the relationship between population and the many different dimensions of development, particularly the environmental dimension, it is essential to distinguish between the various levels of analysis. This is because although globally population's role seems quite secondary, regionally population trends are important but not the only ones involved, and at the local and community level there are not enough studies to enable politically significant lessons to be drawn.[20]

The need to 'integrate population into development' proclaimed at Bucharest in 1974 has proved to be a methodological dead end. It is like an empty shell because it is the result of a political compromise, not a genuine scientific procedure. As Paul Demeny says, in Bucharest

> *'the developing countries' representatives showed little enthusiasm for the quantitative objectives of fertility reduction proposed by a number of industrialized countries. Two major changes were therefore made to the plan to make it accept-*

able to everyone: the quantified objectives were abandoned and the macroeconomic justification for family planning was replaced by reasoning based on human rights. To consolidate everything, the Bucharest agreement stated that population growth and development should be dealt with in an integrated manner, i.e. population policies should not be regarded as substitutes for development but rather as an element to facilitate it.'[21]

According to Jean-Claude Chasteland,[22] the integration concept is still basically unstructured and without much practical value because it is the direct result of the need for the political compromise mentioned above. At the time of the Bucharest Conference, integration was the price to be paid for securing legitimation of fertility reduction policies. Moreover, it was not until 1983 that a technical definition of integration was provided. Today, planning is dead and integration in the technical sense no longer has any practical value.

Economic Growth or Sustainable Societies: the Choice Has to be Made

The final inconsistency is the one governments created in Cairo when they called unanimously for sustained economic growth in the context of the sustainable development of all countries. By setting an objective with two incompatible elements, governments sowed confusion in people's minds.[23] Is a world trade system imaginable in which all countries would have a positive trade balance? The resoundingly affirmed need to achieve sustained economic growth in all countries is evidence of governments' refusal to question the economic system upon which the industrialized countries have founded their prosperity and their advantage over the rest of the world. Thus, the proposed economic framework for solving population problems turns out to be a system in which 'profit seeking is the sole logic, generalized free trade the sole policy, the productivity race the sole formula for efficiency, and wage and employment flexibility the sole social policy'.[24] The other element is education, which Wallerstein says is portrayed as the miraculous remedy for enabling Third World populations to acquire the industrialized world's skills and values which they supposedly need in order to catch up.[25]

Instead of analysing the macroeconomic mechanisms responsible for poverty, states both North and South have agreed to maintain the *status quo*. They prefer to ignore the fact that the North's model is incompatible with sustainability and inappropriate to the South's economic, human and institutional realities (in respect of employment and social welfare, for example). Moreover, in affirming the right to development they have deliberately neglected the difficult issue of potential conflicts between, on the one hand, the North's right to consume and the South's right to have the necessary resources for raising the standard of living, and on the other hand the unflinching determination of the industrialists of the North to export to the South and the urgent need for the South's economies to develop.

United Nations programmes of action adopted since the 1970s, whether for children, the environment, population or social development, are all based on the firm belief that 'development is accessible to everyone if the necessary action is taken' and if adequate resources are devoted to it. The approach predominating in international debates, upon which development assistance strategies are founded, derives directly from the liberal ideology created by the myth surrounding the Industrial Revolution.[26] According to this ideology, there are three spheres of activity: the sphere of the market and economic activity; the sphere of the state and political control; and the private sphere. The system develops on the basis of a norm of change peculiar to industrialized nations and imposed on other countries – namely, progress. Progress is justified on the ground that it eliminates disparities in the distribution of wealth. To overcome underdevelopment is therefore to catch up the industrialized countries through growth – a model that goes hand in hand with the idea of demographic transition and modernization. In reality, however, things happen differently because catching up means competing and ultimately competition implies that one country develops at the expense of another. Furthermore, the egalitarian distribution of growth's benefits has proved illusory: the disparities in wealth have continued to increase both between countries and within countries since the start of the Development Decade.

According to Wallerstein, to overcome the inconsistencies into which the Cairo document's approach leads the discussion, we must 'unthink' social science because its assumptions, inherited from the nineteenth century, prevent a productive analysis of the contemporary world. We must also challenge its most debatable concept – development – by asking ourselves a number of questions. For example, what must be developed in development? Who or what has actually been developed? What is implicitly being called for when development is called for? On what conditions can such development occur? What are the political consequences of the replies to the first four questions?'[27]

In the past, international negotiations were able to narrow these inconsistencies by creating conciliatory notions that proved particularly effective: the notion of responsibility and the notion of integration of population into development. Now, however, the second of these has lost all credibility owing to lack of precision, and so only the ethics of responsibility is left to overcome inconsistencies.

The Demographic Perspective: The Risk of Irrelevance

The Swedish parliamentarian Karl-Göran Biosmark has identified one of the main conclusions prompted by the Programme of Action: the 'new view of demographic development taken by the Cairo Conference deprives population policy of its relevance as a self-contained concept'. In his opinion, 'demographic development is looked on as a consequence of the conditions under which people live and of their needs and environment in the broad sense, not as a policy field in its own right'.[28]

With the removal of all macro (economic, social or political) considerations from the argument, the debate has become a dead end. The Programme of Action on Population enshrines the break between, on the one hand, reproductive health and family planning programmes, which are henceforth justified solely in terms of human rights, and even more so women's rights and social and health needs, and on the other hand considerations which, as the debate stands at present, are no longer related to the demographic perspective or social change. Health and family planning action thus becomes, at least theoretically, independent of demographic purposes (stabilization of the world population). In three decades of international negotiations, family planning has therefore gone from being a means of reducing population growth to an end in itself for reasons of health and well-being. By progressively removing the population perspective's other elements, the structuring of international negotiations around fertility reduction has segmented the debate. Henceforth, it is likely to be divided up into many different fora, as foreshadowed by the call to hold separate international conferences on migration and the elderly. The shrinking of the population perspective carries with it the risk that we shall miss the real challenges of our time. It is to identifying those challenges that the demographic perspective can make a major contribution.

Chapter 7
Coping with the Challenges Facing Us

The challenges facing us become clearer when a distinction is made between inherited and therefore inevitable problems, and those for which there exist preventive measures. Given past trends, we have to expect a world population that will have almost doubled by 2050. Not only is the magnitude of population challenges changing but also their nature, because we now have to think out and structure a sustainable world for tens of billions of human beings. At the heart of the challenges are socioeconomic organization, relations between individuals, generations and peoples, the relationship between man and nature, biodiversity and the diversity of humankind's cultural heritage, as well as other matters. There are no ready-made solutions for these challenges because

> 'this concern for our descendants' well-being can inspire very diverse and even contradictory policies. For example, in the ecology debate, concern for future generations can be invoked in support of an extreme conservationist position, such as 'deep ecology', while at the other end of the spectrum of possible opinions, it can give rise to what are, it must said, fairly technocratic arguments for voluntary-based management of the planet aimed at actively protecting resources and options for the distant future.'[1]

From Population Control to the Transformation of Societies

The new population challenges are less to do with quantitative population growth than with how societies will organize themselves to cope with the transformations they are undergoing. We shall be required to mobilize all our intellectual and organizational capacities to address the complex linkages between population change, the transformation of the economic system, and the evolution of social norms and individual aspirations.

The Course of History: Acceleration, Globalization and Increasing Complexity

Three major trends are emerging: the acceleration of the processes underlying the pattern of living; the integration of the interactions between the various types of phenomena affecting our existence; and the realization that if we are to understand what is happening, we must view phenomena in all their complexity. Population growth is not an isolated phenomenon but part of the deep-seated trend of the main processes at work in shaping our world. Whether it is our ability to explore the infinitely small or the infinitely large, everything is changing at an ever greater speed, 'made possible by the increase in the number of alternatives generated by all forms of life'.[2] The great difficulty which individuals and social institutions have in controlling the changes is undoubtedly the cause of the present disorder.

Our history, however, is neither linear nor sequential: it contains numerous breaks that mark the thresholds in the increasing complexity both of forms of life and in the relations between the different orders of living creatures. Realization of environmental degradation has caused us to reflect on the relationship between the economic logic we pursue and changes in the ecological balance upon which mankind's survival depends. Social crises, conflicts of all sorts and the ensuing wars clearly indicate that the individual, sociocultural and macroeconomic dimensions of our collective future are now closely interlinked. Similarly, the globalization of markets – with the exchange of goods and capital movements involved – and the movement of people make it impossible now to view change factors in isolation, outside the very broad context affecting them.

The history of humankind, and of its technology and institutions, reveals a succession of transitions of various sorts which, ever since *Homo erectus* appeared, have continued to radically change his mode of interaction with the world and his fellow beings. Globalization requires first and foremost a new

131

Annual growth rate

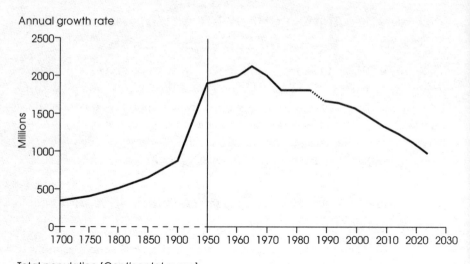

Total population [*Continental curve*]

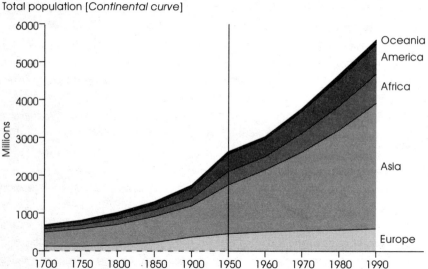

Sources: David Reher; UN Population Division

Figure 7.1 *World Population Growth*

perspective for interrelating all these factors. It testifies to increased economic and political interdependence, compelling states to reconsider certain of their privileges in the light of universal challenges which only supranational institutions can regulate in the collective interest. The speed at which developments occur and the integration of phenomena require new principles for understanding our history. Not only is everything changing much faster but also everything seems to be becoming increasingly diversified, so much so that the simple models used to describe our development are now obsolete. How can we explain these breaks in our development and these abrupt changes in the direction taken by a phenomenon other than by acknowledging that we are in a stage of profound change where processes suddenly start to follow a pattern unlike the familiar one? Since the quantitative conditions defining our system have changed, it is now changing qualitatively. Population growth is an example of such change.

These new realities place us in what Isabelle Stengers calls 'a situation of complexity', i.e. a situation in which a particular way of doing things can no longer be continued on the basis of a simple time-honoured model, a situation in which new questions have to asked. According to her,[3] we are entering an intellectually aware but perplexed period, since we now see that human histories and the histories of the climate, epidemics, diseases, explorations and lifestyles form an inseparable whole. Cognitively speaking, we are therefore in a situation which makes us aware that the responses we arrive at depend first and foremost on the way problems are presented. Complexity should not be expected to provide answers and paradigms, or to be a theory in itself. What it suggests are new questions and requirements, not new positive components of knowledge. Complexity does not constitute the possibility of a new unity of knowledge – quite the contrary. It introduces the idea that above all we must think about the limits to scientific method, certainty, types of scientific modes of representation and simple concepts. At best, it can reveal a world that has had a number of different histories, crises and abrupt changes.

Reviewing Humankind's Place in the Economic System

The demographic perspective enables us to assess fully the implications of the economic system that has predominated, to various degrees and at various rates, since the Industrial Revolution. 'The core of the social issue today [is] once again the existence of useless individuals and supernumeraries, and around them a cluster of situations in which the future is both precarious and uncertain, indicating an upsurge in mass vulnerability'.[4] The stupendous productivity increase due to technology now makes human beings less and less necessary in the production process. At the same time, the nature of the predominant form of economic activity is changing: the production of goods is being supplanted by service activities, even in the agricultural and industrial sectors. This transitional phase, which is marked by all kinds of uncertainties and dysfunctions, is causing mass unemployment in the industrialized countries. If the same pattern is reproduced in the South – and there is no reason to suppose otherwise – unemployment, which economically speaking may be

likened to relative overpopulation, will rise still further because of these countries' population dynamics. If the economy and technology are allowed to
dictate the rules, then every country already has 'excess human beings'. The
risk is that populations' economic situation will marginalize people without
jobs (not only the unemployed but also the elderly, people with disabilities and
so on), and at the same time exploit the most vulnerable individuals, particularly women and children, to the full. No country is spared the erosion of
employment and no social group can claim to be free from insecurity, because
poverty troubles the conscience even of those with a guaranteed income.

Although methods for assessing ecological capital deterioration are being
developed, there are currently two serious deficiencies – lack of attention to
the dwindling of currently available human capital, and lack of vision regarding the need to invest in human capital as yet unborn. These are all the more
serious since in the North profound social changes involve a radical change in
outlook regarding economic and social objectives to be pursued, while in the
South only the healthiest and best educated human resources are in a position
to create the conditions for sustainable development. Starting from the principle that 'social matters are not a pale imitation of economic matters',[5] we
may ask ourselves: in the present economic situation, 'what will be the demographic responses of social groups and families? How will demographic
systems integrate the new survival strategies? In a situation of strong demographic pressure, will the decline in living conditions, health and education
slow down demographic transition or speed it up?'.[6]

We are on the threshold of potential changes that could provide 20 per
cent of the world's population with a better quality of life, while 80 per cent
would revert to conditions that are best not described. On the basis of per
capita income growth, René Passet[7] distinguishes three groups of countries
likely to evolve differently. The population of the first group – the highly
industrialized countries – lives in a world where the satisfaction of material
needs is nearing saturation point and demand is tending towards other, less
material satisfactions such as health, leisure and culture. In the second group
– the newly industrialized countries – the population aspires to live in a region
of resources and material comfort where the accumulation of consumer
durables such as domestic appliances and a car holds sway. In the third group
the population exists on the bare minimum. Daily life in those countries is
dominated by the sheer need to survive, food consumption being most important of all.

Given the forces at work, there is the possibility that the three socioeconomic systems represented by those groups of countries may go their separate
ways. The first system would lead to a better quality of life for the population

---

In the news

In Shaba, a Return to the Stone Age

The 500-kilometre dirt road from Lubumbashi to Lake Moero is one of the main routes for transporting fish caught in the lake and the region's agricultural produce. For the last three years, however, the Highways Department, nicknamed here the Potholes Department, has not been maintaining it... Employees have not seen a payslip for three years... As a result, essential goods have become exceedingly scarce throughout the region... The Upper Lomani has reverted to the Stone Age... The bluish foam from papaya leaves is used as soap, but it damages clothes and causes skin irritations. For night-time lighting, the umwenge tree replaces the hurricane lamp and oil... But the smoke it produces gives the peasants red eyes like witches. To light a fire now, you have to be dexterous. Because there are no matches, you set fire to wood shavings by rapidly turning a lushiko stick on a small board made of very hard wood... As for salt, there is none available or if there is, it is too expensive... Harvests cannot be cleared because the roads are not maintained. Successive monetary reforms and hyperinflation − 30 000 per cent since October 1993 − penalize the peasants, whose savings lose their value within a few days because they are unable to exchange their banknotes in time.

Bethuel Kasamwa Tuseko, La Référence Plus/Syfia,
February 1995, Kinshasa

---

of the industrialized countries. The second would make maximum use of its populations' economic potential for the sole purpose of material development. The third system would be totally unable by itself to set in train the economic development process. Sooner or later, there might be a real decline in the economic and demographic indicators of well-being; in fact, this is already happening in several regions of the world. How would we cope with that? Either we accept that there are humans and subhumans, and that a minority of affluent people consume for their own well-being the resources that the majority need in order to live. Or we must redefine the rules on the basis of the principle that every human being already born or yet to be born has the right to a decent life, and we must agree to pay whatever that may cost.

From Policy-making to Decision-making

'Every action and every decision...implies choice and renunciation, i.e. reference to something better whose definition is ultimately founded on a conception of man and the world.'[8] There are two critical thresholds in international action. The first of these is crossed when negotiating succeeds

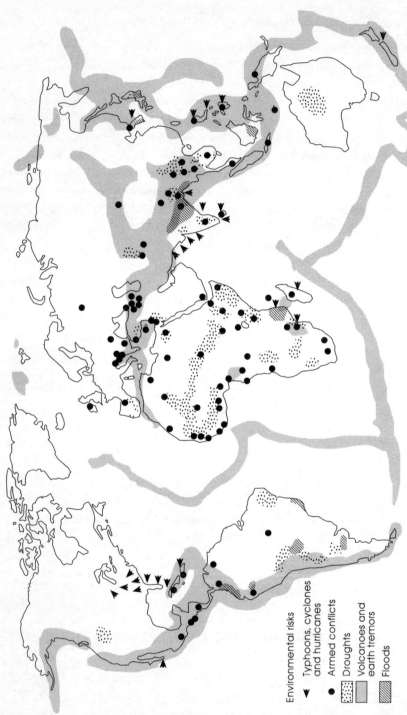

Figure 7.2 *Danger Areas*

in reconciling all the interests involved and results in jointly agreed positions. The second threshold, which is a practical one, separates the main decision-making principles. It is crucial because it separates theory from practice, and political statement from the actual improvement of individual living conditions.

As in the other major United Nations documents of the 1990s, human beings are the chief concern of the Programme of Action on Population. Specifically, this means that demographic facts and emerging trends must serve as a framework for rethinking the desired socioeconomic structure, i.e. sustainable local, regional and international development. Since sustainable development 'is defined with reference to maintaining or increasing human well-being, three approaches are theoretically possible, depending on whether this well-being's economic, ecological or social aspects are emphasized'.[9] Neither an economic nor an ecological solution, however, can deal with inevitable future population growth because according to both economic and ecological criteria today's world is already overpopulated. The social solution is therefore potentially the only one compatible with a minimalist ethical position which maintains that the two to four billion human beings that will inevitably be added to the world population over the next fifty years have not only the right to exist but also the right to a decent life. This position implies that a solution will not be found unless economic requirements are redefined on the basis of demographic realities (in all their diversity) in order to ensure the well-being of eight to ten billion people, with respect for ecological balance. Such an approach differs radically from population policies, which were based on the opposite reasoning. Their aim was to make population trends compatible with the economic criteria for well-being as defined by the dominant economic system.

Given current population trends and on the basis of the principles set by the international community, it is necessary to rethink many aspects of the economic and social system: the definition of productive activities, the nature of wealth, women's participation in reproduction and production, the compatibility of parental and work roles with individual aspirations, time management, income and social security policies, and generally the structuring of the economy to enhance as much as possible each country's demographic potential (for example, elderly people in the industrialized countries and young people in the developing economies). This sort of rethinking, which has reached different stages in different countries, is only just beginning internationally. We shall therefore confine ourselves here to exploratory discussions aimed at providing some different lines of thought that will contribute to the ongoing debate.

There is No Job Problem

There is nothing more absurd than wanting to create jobs. Wanting to generate income and sources of income: salaries, monthly payments, allowances, annuities, pensions, social (or unsocial!) security... Wanting to create consumer goods ... bread, toasters, rolls, bicycles, perfumes, maps of exotic countries, houses, lipstick... Wanting to create services – nothing is more natural than all that, nothing is wiser than all that ... post offices and travel agencies ... schools, hospitals ... evening trains... But wanting to create jobs? Jobs are a only means... It is ends that have to be pursued... There is no job problem. There is an income problem and a time problem. Actually, it is a lack-of-income problem: no one knows where to find this income. And it is a too-much-time problem: no one knows what to do with all this time. A money-related problem, and a use-of-time problem. The first is economic, the second ontological. Both are metaphysical. The economic problem takes the form of a quest; the ontological problem, the form of an ordeal.

Renaud Camus, POL, Paris, 1994

The first line of thought, suggested by Gonzague Pillet, is of a theoretical nature. His purpose may seem surprising to people who are not economists. It is, however, more practical than might be imagined, as his ideas are being given effect to in the international climate change negotiations. First, he spells out the value judgments underlying the way population trends are viewed and therefore determining the decision-making framework within which solutions have to be found to the problems posed by those trends. Next, he clarifies current demographic challenges and shows why international negotiations must move from the present approach, based on the individual optimization criterion, to a procedural and collective approach. Lastly, he attempts to conceptualize the point at which states' political principles intersect with the economic machinery for their implementation.

The Economic Decision-making Framework
Gonzague Pillet

Implicit Value Judgments

The dominant economic model makes individual preferences the foundation of rational economic decisions. However democratic it may appear initially, this foundation is unsuitable for taking account of population-related phenomena. Making a decision means choosing from among a limited number of actions the one that will lead to the

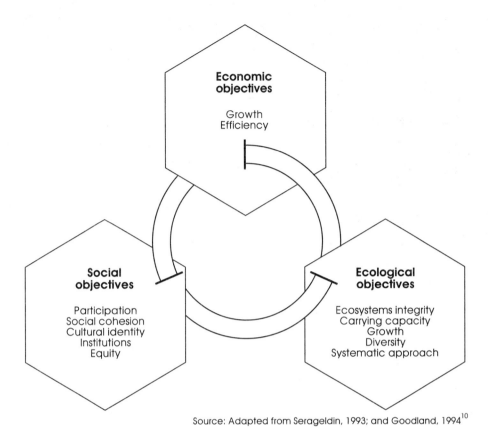

Source: Adapted from Serageldin, 1993; and Goodland, 1994[10]

Figure 7.3 *Beyond Economic Objectives*

best possible result. This assumes that only the decision-maker is involved and that he or she has well-defined objectives. 'The' solution will be the one best able to meet those objectives. However, when the decision is about population and quality of life options, it is impossible to envisage a result that is optimal in relation to all possible perspectives – social, cultural, environmental and economic. Thus no option meets the criterion of 'the' best response. Consequently, the decision-making framework can no longer be founded upon a strictly individual optimization criterion.

Under the dominant economic model, the individual makes choices on the basis of expected future utility. By referring to utility it is possible to move from an objective level (financial gain related to a precise objective) to a more subjective one (satisfaction derived). In a situation of uncertainty and/or risk, the individual decision-maker substitutes the notion of utility for the monetary assessment of the final result, i.e. a function of the final result. This utilitarian shortcut does not work, however, for decisions relating to society as a whole, since well-being does not exist as a social function.[11] Such a function could of course be imposed dictatorially, but it could not be created by rational means. In other words, there is no link between individual satisfaction and societal satisfaction insofar as social well-being cannot be defined without reference to individual satisfaction. A number of challenges, however, require this fundamental normative principle to be transcended. Thus, in view of long-term and uncertain global challenges such as population challenges, it is impossible to optimize an economic decision on a strictly demographic basis. The problem lies not so much in conceiving of an optimum as in the fact that such an optimum, for which there may be various options, quite simply cannot be defined in practice. The characteristics of worldwide demographic change – the subject of international negotiations – therefore compel us to choose another decision-making framework.

A New Approach to Negotiations

Demographic change requires a decision-making framework able to take account of at least four factors:

1. the global nature of the phenomenon;
2. its scale, i.e. its absolute numbers;
3. the time span over which phenomena's significance becomes clear (several generations), which exceeds the customary economic time span (between 1 and approximately 15 years); and
4. the degree of uncertainty and risk attached to demographic change and to the impacts of demographic parameters. Demographic change is global in the sense that each separate individual contributes to the general pattern. According to a strict economic definition, population trends produce negative or positive externalities affecting both individual well-being and business profits, without any compensation between agents. These externalities are themselves global insofar as there is *a priori* no material or instant possibility of compensation between individual agents, since all of them both cause and suffer such effects. At the level of a larger entity, this means that a country by itself can have only a marginal impact on the general situation, even though doing something would finally have substantially altered its demographic importance.

The inconsistency between the dominant economic reasoning and population trends (maximization of individual utility – *optimum optimorum*) therefore leads us to seek a model other than individual compensation. The idea underlying economic reasoning does not require a compensation to the letter, but in spirit. If the gains of those who benefit from transition to a new economic state can compensate, at least theoretically, the losses sustained by the others, the new state can be regarded as optimal within Pareto's meaning.[12] Thus, the growth stabilization objective set by one country requires that an identical objective be set by the agents of all, or nearly all, other countries.[13] Furthermore, the global nature of the population issue makes the quality of life associated with different demographic situations a commodity that is not merely public, but *internationally public*. That implies, for instance, a new approach to property rights, issue rights and trade and technology transfers between countries with different levels of development, as well as a fresh analysis of economic tools. Deciding on options for making a particular quality of life universal and lasting implies, therefore, that choices must be made collectively. Deciding means assessing the challenges of different possible scenarios and classifying them on a rational basis. Deciding collectively means delegating to international negotiation – and no longer to individuals alone – the responsibility for assessing the challenges and for classifying them according to collectively agreed criteria.[14] This is what is called the search for 'global accord'.[15] There are two possibilities: procedure-based decision-making and collective decision-making accompanied by negotiation. Whereas economic decision-making seeks the best response to a particular question (optimization), procedure-based decision-making focuses on how to take the right decision, with particular emphasis on the decision-making process rather than what is actually decided. Collective decision-making, on the other hand, is mostly about risk-sharing, i.e. negotiating the outcome of the decision and the possibilities for sharing the risks among the parties concerned. These different decision-making frameworks interact, and fit one within the other like Russian dolls. An individual may still seek to optimize his or her decisions but will do so within the framework of a procedure and a collective model negotiated among the parties.

Table 7.1 *Types of Negotiation*

Decision-making models	Objectives and mechanisms
Individual optimization	Determining through cost–benefit analysis the best response for maximizing expected utility on the basis of an efficiency criterion.
Procedure-based	Drawing up the rules of procedure for reaching a decision based on broad acceptance of its implications.
Collective	Risk-sharing; determining the extent of responsibilities and assessing the outcome as a subject for the negotiation itself.

The Economic Tools for Making Choices

Externalities are not only global but also intergenerational, and thus demographic phenomena's timescale presents economic reasoning and conventional analytical tools with a new challenge. Indeed, the intergenerational dimension is a considerable difficulty in international negotiations.

In the area of population policy, the cost of prevention falls to the present generation, although few individuals or groups derive any benefit from its investment diverted from other possible uses for consumption or production. At the very most, each is a loser 'non-trivially', whereas future generations would be the winners because of damage avoided.[16] Economically speaking, it is therefore a matter of transferring the present generation's real well-being to future generations to offset the damage that current activities may do to those generations. On the one hand, we may therefore say that all countries must take coordinated preventive action, in the knowledge however that countries differ greatly in their willingness to make such a sacrifice, particularly for resource endowment, economic growth and human capital reasons. On the other hand, we may ask whether a prevention policy can be economically attractive. Where rapid demographic change is concerned, short-term costs are much more important than expected long-term benefits, and will always be so. Even with a low discount rate, the benefits of preventive measures will never be as great as their cost.

Discounting is not the only element in economic analysis as applied to demographic change: uncertainty and risk are two other major ones. At the strictly economic level, uncertainty and risk may be treated in a standard fashion when agents, who possess reliable information, are deemed to be capable of managing a specific problem. This is not so, however, regarding demographic change, which is marked by great uncertainty and collective risks.[17] Because of their characteristics, none of demographic change's components can be reduced to each other and the normal probabilistic treatment cannot therefore be applied to them. Moreover, it appears that the treatment of great uncertainty leads to a situation comparable to the discount situation since it introduces a considerable bias in relation to long periods of time.[18] Indeed, present consumption would increase as a reaction to great uncertainty caused by non-additive probabilities, thus destroying the possibilities of investing in the future. In economic terms, patience would consist in waiting for better information to become available before taking a decision. Normally, more information should remove uncertainty. Economics recognizes such a phenomenon since it attaches a value to information not yet available. In the case of demographic change, however, waiting to be able to remove the inherent uncertainty of demographic trends before taking action is out of the question, because of the substantial time difference between the point at which a new trend is clearly perceived and the point at which its effects begin to be felt. Furthermore, owing to the complexity of the parameters involved and of their evolution over a long period, the information's relative value is not great, since uncertainty cannot be expected to be removed in the short term.

These considerations should prevail in long-term decisions. Investments related to future generations should be the subject of unconventional economic analyses. An example is Rothenberg's recommendation that the principle of backward indebtedness be applied. In his view, instead of regarding the present generation as having an altruistic responsibility to future generations, we should regard it as owing a debt to the past – to previous generations and to nature. He thus puts forward the idea that the possibilities available to the present generation derive largely from the inheritance bequeathed by previous generations and from the work of nature itself. This memory – we may think here of the energy memory of ecological networks[19] – could be transmitted as a post-payment to future generations rather than being

---

The Value of Life: A Statistical Approach

The statistical value of life is an economic concept defined as the value which a person in a statistically defined population assigns to a modified death risk. Clearly, the figures given here are theoretical and are not an estimate of life's intrinsic value, which cannot differ from one place to another.

In international negotiations, the statistical value of life will differ, depending on whether it is calculated on the basis of the sociodemographic parameters of the countries of the North or of the South. By way of example, on the basis of current parameters the statistical value of life is put at $1.5 million for the countries of the North and at $0.1 million for the countries of the South. Where international comparisons are concerned, it is difficult to refer to a purely economic decision-making framework (optimum of the statistical value of life). Consequently, these values have to be 'negotiated' using a collective decision-making framework.

---

payable to previous generations, such payment being impossible in practice. The present generation would therefore offer the next generation the right to begin its existence with at least the same potential as it had when it began its own existence.

Economic Implementation Mechanisms

The market today is an unavoidable reality. Markets, however, can change, whether they are financial or insurance markets. If criteria are redefined, markets can offer useful solutions to the problem of demographic change and quality of life.[20] The market's advantage is that it involves a genuine economic commitment that can compel countries to act in accordance with their positions of principle at international conferences.

The main factors likely to enter into market logic are the degree of risk aversion, the discount rate and 'Arrow's securities'.[21] Risk aversion and the discount rate act in opposite directions in relation to the willingness to deprive oneself of part of one's income in order to avoid risks. The greater the fear of risk, the more a country, for example, will be inclined to insure itself against threats to the natural environment and the economy due to demographic pressure. On the other hand, the higher the discount rate, the more the future will lose in terms of importance. Consequently, different countries may have different attitudes towards preventive demographic investments. Why not open the betting and put on the market Arrow's securities, whose purpose would be to ensure consistency between countries' intentions and their investments to give effect to those intentions?

'Arrow's securities' are bonds which would pay out if and only if, on the agreed due date, a particular state in the population–standard of living ratio was confirmed

– namely, the one on which a specific country or group of countries had made wagers, some betting on slight damage to the quality of life, others on substantial damage. The country paying out would be the risk's country of origin, while the securities buyer would be the country wanting to insure itself against risk. In the event of a bad result for a country of origin, the countries that bought the securities would acquire through the market the means of coping with the negative impacts of the other countries' non-responsibility (for example, refugee flows, substantial increased economic migration, etc.). Eventually, there could be considerable regional financial transfers. Meanwhile, the international markets would deal in the securities for amounts likely to total hundreds of billions of dollars. Various new developments, particularly in the field of climate change and insurance, indicate that the market and economic analysis are very flexible and may perhaps prove more effective than strictly political negotiations. However, at the technical level, solutions of this sort are valid – for the moment at least – for only part of the world.

Integration of demographic factors into an economic decision-making framework requires the adoption of a multidimensional framework based on an approach that is both consequential (economic and individual) and procedural (collective and negotiated). Decisions must be framed by global agreements whose main instruments are international negotiations and market mechanisms. To transcend ideology, the decision-making framework must result in a genuine economic choice in the context of a global situation, which is evolving over a long period of time and relates to individuals and countries widely different in terms of culture and resources. Moreover, decisions cannot be taken once and for all, and be claimed to apply to the whole of the next millennium. On the contrary, they must be taken sequentially and integrate the new information that will undoubtedly become available. Similarly, decisions must result in a range of strategies because there cannot be a single strategy for achieving society's objectives, since one body alone cannot decide on the best possible option.

The second line of thought is a practical one. Walter Stahel outlines what can and what must be done immediately by Northern countries to ensure their own responsibility in coping with world population changes. Their main responsibility is to give developing economies enough room to manoeuvre in order to improve the living standards of their populations without causing too much damage to themselves and to the planet. Northern countries must therefore implement new economic strategies, essentially by changing goods production and use standards while keeping with the principles of social, ecological and economic sustainability. What are involved here are specific policies that are being tested in various parts of the world in order to resolve problems identified. These new economic procedures are a step forward in the attempt to cope with unavoidable world population growth. This involves making the best use of available human and natural resources as part of equitable international relations, and avoiding ecological damage.

The New Production of Goods and Standards of Utilization
Walter R. Stahel

The Four Pillars of Sustainability

An economy that is socially and ecologically sustainable both locally and internationally has four pillars:

1. respect for ecological balance (for example, biodiversity and the water cycle);
2. keeping within the toxicity threshold which if exceeded will endanger nature's and mankind's health (qualitative approach);
3. the quest for maximum resource productivity to reduce the flow of resources for meeting human needs (quantitative approach); and
4. social cohesion and cultural attitudes, which determine individual social integration and wish fulfilment capacity.

The first has to do with nature conservation, the second with legislation and technological progress. The third relates to the reorientation of business strategies in a service-focused market economy, which is distinctively different from the present industrial economy. The last is the prerequisite for the other three. It is founded on the social pattern which each human group establishes for itself and its descendants on the basis of its historical conception of mankind. Reorganization of the production and utilization of goods on the basis of those four pillars, and in a spirit of global sustainability, requires new objectives for the economic system.

Some Objectives of a Sustainable Economy

- To create the highest possible utilization value over the longest period of time, with the lowest possible resource and energy consumption.
- To give the South's economies the possibility and ecological room for manoeuvre to increase the resource flows for producing the infrastructures and goods needed to improve their populations' living standards.
- To optimize the management of existing wealth; this wealth, or heritage, is the total of material and non-material resources, goods and skills with or without monetary value. In that sense, every country possesses wealth and the difference between rich and poor countries is no longer meaningful: there are only countries that have put their wealth to good use and those that have not.
- To create meaningful jobs.
- To create goods and services that use primarily renewable local resources to improve the quality of life.
- To reduce raw material depletion from, and discharges into, the biosphere.

The Myth of the Asian Miracle

Helmut Laumer ... of the German research institute IFO started the idea that Asian economic growth has its limits when he said that 'even in Asia economic expansion will not last for ever'. He bases his argument on several factors, including insufficient infrastructure, labour shortages and high inflation. There are a multitude of telecommunications and transport projects in the Asian countries, which do indeed considerably lag behind in terms of infrastructure. However, according to the Asian Development Bank, they will require an investment of at least 1000 billion dollars between now and the year 2000, otherwise growth will fall...

Labour shortages also impact negatively on the region's rapid expansion. 'In Thailand, only about 3000 students a year graduate from technical institutions, and even if new schools are built, it will be thirty to forty years before the effect is felt', says the Thai Development Research Institute...

In the long term, the shortage of energy resources may also hamper growth. 'For China to maintain an annual 10 per cent growth rate, it would have to import 80 per cent of world oil production in 2030, which is impossible', said William Klein, an economist at the American World Economy Research Institute... Environmental degradation is also increasingly impacting on the economy... The newly industrialized countries' economies are now coming of age. Even though it is normal for their growth to start tapering off as Japan's did in the 1970s, the uncertainties about their future are certainly much greater.

Haruo Ozaki, Nihon Keizai Shimbun, *February 1995, Tokyo*

Principles

The guiding principles of the new means of producing and utilizing goods are founded upon two criteria for measuring the desired ends – namely, human well-being and sustainable resource use. There is currently no entirely satisfactory human well-being indicator, although the sustainable economic well-being index (or Genuine Program Indicator in the US) developed two decades ago endeavours to take into account several important elements of the two criteria.

The industrialized countries' economies and the very varied economies of the countries of the South require different changes. In the industrialized countries, the first major principle consists in moving from an industrial economy based on added value to a service economy based on resource management. This requires a product-focused sustainability strategy, i.e. a techno-economic 'dematerialization' – and utilization-oriented strategy as opposed to a production-oriented one. Such a strategy gives precedence to product-life extension (re-using and repairing goods) over recycling. In production – building work, for instance – three-quarters of total

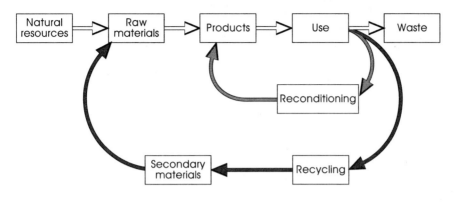

Source: Walter R. Stahel

Figure 7.4 *Closed-loop Production Cycle*

energy and one quarter of total labour input are used in manufacturing materials (steel and concrete, for example), whereas one quarter of total energy and three-quarters of total labour input are used for manufacturing goods. When repair work is undertaken (which is similar in character to the manufacturing of goods), labour is substituted for energy. A sustainable economy must be based on the utilization value of goods, not their exchange value, and maximize that utilization value with the lowest possible resource consumption over longer periods of time. Under this approach economic success is no longer associated with resource flow as is the case in the industrial economy. Resource productivity can increased by reducing the volume and speed of resource flows in the economy.

The second major principle consists in replacing resources and energy by local labour. This is well suited to an economy that devotes more time to maintaining a stock of existing goods (and thus of existing values) in good working order than to producing new goods. Implementing this principle increases the number of meaningful jobs and reduces pollution.

The third principle consists in producers' assuming full responsibility for their products. This forces them to defray the costs related to the life cycle of goods from cradle to grave, the aim being to internalize the end-of-life costs of goods within their production costs. This new economic approach, which is an attempt to optimize wealth within Aristotle's meaning, i.e. enjoyment and non-possession, consumption and destruction, presupposes freedom from the linear production, use and waste model that still affects our way of thinking. It is then realized that it is the utilization, not the production, of goods that bestows a value upon them. The rules for running the economy should therefore consist in optimizing utilization (i.e. performance) and in selling it for the longest possible period of time, with the aim of guaranteeing the customer's satisfaction (still subjective). Consequently, the producer's role is radically changed: he now becomes a service manager, optimizing a stock of goods. The consumer's role also changes: he becomes a user. And the tradesman becomes an adviser/repair man.

147

Methods

For those industrialized countries in which the population is relatively stable and the markets are saturated, the main methods for implementing a new production and utilization strategy are based on the following:

- to seek the highest resource productivity so as to provide the same level of well-being with a tenth of current material inputs (i.e. a reduction by a factor of 10);
- to extend the useful life of materials and goods as long as possible through a modular system design concept, and using standardized components;
- to 'dematerialize' products in order to decrease resource flows, i.e. reducing the relative importance of the materials in a product's composition in comparison with other inputs such as information;
- to create multifunctional products;
- to find systemic solutions through replacing the linear production–utilization–waste economy by an economy in loops based on utilization value;
- to decentralize the economy (services, remanufacturing, recycling, research and management) through the creation of small regional bodies that will make good use of the existing stock of goods, know-how and local resources, use more and better-qualified labour, reduce the volume of goods transported and increase the flow of immaterial goods (information);
- to move from an economy based on the mobility of workers to a mobility of the workplace;
- to flexibilize work organization so as to take account of the fact that a service economy must operate 24 hours a day, seven days a week, without however impacting negatively on workers' quality of life – quite the contrary.

Conditions and Means

The legislation, production structures and tax systems inherited from the economic logic of the past need to be adapted to the new requirements. Long-term product optimization requires preventive engineering, modular construction, standardized components, risk management and programmed preventive maintenance. Maintenance quality is becoming as important as production quality, if not more so. The sustainability strategy uses the same methods and reaches the same conclusions as risk management: loss prevention and waste reduction are cheaper than repairs or waste disposal. It is thus better to maintain what already exists than to produce something new. Here are a few examples. High-quality long-life goods (some of the best examples of which are compact discs and low-energy-consumption lamps) have a long life because they are 'stand-alone' solutions. For more complex products, it is the product's conception and modular construction, with its standardized and inter-compatible components, which can be adapted to new technology and changing user needs that make it a long-life good. As a result, the entire product's life can be extended through the exchange of components (for example, bicycles, planes and photocopiers). There are different ways of extending the life of a product and its components: local re-use (for instance, glass bottles and items bought at a fleamarket); local repairs (e.g. cars that have been involved in an accident); remanufacturing in regional centres (e.g. typewriter ribbon recolouring, tyre retreading); and technological upgrading (external insulation of an existing building, computer upgrading). Used items can be utilized again through a 'cascading' system for less demanding functions (for instance, an express train's locomotive could be used to tow goods trains and could end its life as a shunting engine). Lastly, utilization can be optimized by service companies which sell utilization of a product (for example, towels, apartments and car rentals) or a system performance (for example, linen for hotel restaurants, railways and telecommunications companies).

Obstacles

There are many obstacles to the adoption of new production and utilization standards. Current technical standards relate to the nature of materials and not their performance (result). Component remanufacturing technology is insufficiently developed. There are no early-warning systems to prevent breakdowns or defects in components. Legal guarantee requirements are generally short term. Consumer protection laws are unsatisfactory – for example, the requirement that products have to be made of new components, rather than having to be products with high-quality components. The used products and components market is still very limited, owing to a lack of people able to determine a product's remaining life. The training of repair and maintenance engineers is hardly organized. Few manufacturers have a knowledge of risk management or manufacture repairable products. Changes in production methods cause conflicts of interest: many manufacturers prefer a linear economy because it is what they know and what is most profitable and/or presents the least risk. Finally, the way value is calculated should be reviewed; it should be based on a product's utilization or replacement value, not only on tax depreciation.

The consumer society's dominant values are without doubt the greatest obstacle to rethinking the way the economy is run. The quality criterion and the value attached to a product's durability are not part of socially dominant criteria. On the contrary, the consumer society values what is brand new, novel and therefore short-lived. Changing these criteria requires a change of paradigm.[22] Since the socially dominant values are linked to ownership of goods, and not the enjoyment derived from them, they are at variance with sharing, solidarity and the concept of usufruct underlying the principle of intergenerational equity. We must abandon the possession/production–destruction equation and return to the resource enjoyment and wealth management equation. Transformation of the industrialized countries' economic system is essential not only for ensuring that the ecological balance is maintained but also for enabling all countries to participate equally in developing their own resources. In particular, this involves the North's transfer of production capacity to the South, i.e. the transfer of capital, energy and technology.

Pillet's theoretical reflections and Stahel's practical steps are significant in that they identify solutions other than merely reducing the fertility of the countries of the South to population-related realities and trends. Pillet suggests another way of negotiating and assuming collective responsibility, while Stahel proposes a different economic structure based on developing human capital and maximizing resource productivity. Problems are therefore reformulated in ethical, not demographic, terms. Because of the potential conflicts in a country between individual interests and collective well-being, and the conflict between the right of the industrialized countries' populations to consume and the right of the populations of the South to have the necessary resources for improving their standard of living, each of those issues involves dilemmas that nowadays emerge in the field of ethics. This indicates that we have reached the point at which, in the words of Paul Ricoeur, 'politics becomes rooted in ethics: the ethics of a people's desire to live together'.[23]

Conclusion:
Population as an Ethical Issue

Ethical issues arise in current debates because, for one reason, we are at a turning point in history where 'human beings may be individually innocent and collectively responsible, all culprits and victims at the same time'.[1] Many population-related subjects raise fundamental ethical questions. Unfortunately, however, the 1994 Cairo population negotiations did not deal with those subjects from an ethical standpoint. This was because before discussing objectives, government representatives made maintaining their value system the precondition for endorsing the Programme of Action. In so doing, they ensured that unlike binding collective standards, it was not prescriptive. By declaring at the outset that 'The implementation of the recommendations contained in the Programme of Action is the sovereign right of each country, consistent with national laws and development priorities, with full respect for the various religious and ethical values and cultural backgrounds of its people', states refused to endorse universal standards supplanting their religious dogmas and cultural particularities. This cautiousness may well express states' legitimate concern to protect themselves against population policy imperialism. The fact remains, however, that such a framework prevented the debate from going beyond already recognized human rights principles.

The Ethical Quest

There are three reasons why population cannot be discussed today without reference to ethics. First, the consensus that made religious dogma both the basis for interpreting individual and social standards and the source of such standards no longer exists. Because there are many different intellectual systems and because human beings are seeking answers to new problems, old standards are no longer enough. Human relations and the relationship between mankind and nature are moving the debate in new directions, which a host of ethics committees and studies are now trying to clarify. Second, there is a growing gulf between science and morality, which bioethics is making more palpable.[2] Third, ethics is a necessary background to the debate because choices have to be made and because only ethics provides a basis for those choices we shall have to make to ensure the future of both humankind and the planet (assuming, of course, we believe the human race must survive). Neither science nor economics can provide an answer to this issue because 'life implies an immanent purpose, but purpose is not a category of understanding, and therefore not a scientific category. This makes it impossible to provide an objective scientific demonstration of a natural purpose'.[3]

The Ethical Dimension

Since ethics is 'that which imposes a responsibility for those who are subject to our power',[4] the exercise of this responsibility in the area of population has many ramifications. First, ethics assigns responsibility for present generations. How is account to be taken of the differences between individuals (people with disabilities, individuals who are ineffectual according to prevailing criteria) and between cultures? How is one to reconcile the different values involved in individual and collective choices? What is the justification for choosing one option rather than another? The population debate's ethical dimension serves first and foremost to put that question into perspective. It raises two issues: the human cost of development and the pursuit of excellence, both of which emerge from the trends discussed by the international community.

Second, ethics compels us to consider collective responsibility for future generations, because the social choices made today will inevitably impact on our descendants' lives. In that connection, Dieter Birnbacher[5] highlights several preliminary questions: how is one to define the right of future generations when, to be applicable, a right needs a vehicle, i.e. a subject? A subject that exists only potentially cannot have a moral right, not even the right to exist. Existence is therefore presupposed in attributing a right and cannot become the content of a right. From what stage are future generations future; in other words, for which generations is the present generation responsible?

How far does responsibility for the unborn go? Moreover, can our criteria adequately assess the world's future states, particularly since many factors – notably our emotional preferences – affect our judgment? Those preferences incline us towards the present and towards what is nearest us in human terms. Lastly, the ethical dimension raises the central issue of the choice between maximizing individual benefit with no regard for the collective interest, and seeking to ensure satisfactory living conditions for the vast majority of people on the basis of equity.

Looking to the future, Hans Jonas offers more food for thought. He calls on us to get rid of everything that could stand in the way of what is now known as ecological sustainability, stressing the need to carefully consider our choices in the light of the precautionary principle. In so doing, he proposes nothing short of an epistemological revolution:

> '*According to Descartes, to determine what is indubitably true we must regard all that which in one way or another can be doubted as equivalent to what has been demonstrated to be false. Here, on the contrary, we must treat as a certainty for decision-making purposes that which can of course be doubted, while being possible, as from when it is a possibility of a certain type*'.[6]

Many factors are impediments to what Jonas calls for, and two in particular. The first is the ideology of progress, which has given rise to the belief that humankind's dynamism can solve all problems. The second is the predominance of short-term political interests, which are incompatible with investing in the future. 'The future has no vote!'[7] Nevertheless, according to Monique Castillo, the success of Jonas' analysis lies in his theorization of the fragility of nature understood in terms of responsibility. 'Fragile is that to which anything can be done and whose being, including continued being, is entirely our responsibility. For those who have nothing there remains only ethics to authorize them in their being',[8] hence the need to reflect on giving, for it 'is the luxury of an unfettered relationship with other people which makes ethics a vital disposition in its own right'.[9]

The Ethical Crisis

Because of these many questions, the fragility of value judgments and the uncertainty of all action appear in a new light, and one may rightly speak of a crisis in this area. The social crisis in many countries is perhaps merely a consequence of the doubts about the legitimacy of current ethical judgments. According to Dominique Folscheid, the present-day crisis is characterized by the fact that

From Eldorado to Chaos

Here, in the days of oil and easy living, even slum dwellers used to drink Scotch whisky. Homes where they did not drink good brands were beyond the pale. Nowadays, despite the crisis, television still hounds the people in poor areas (and elsewhere), encouraging them to overconsume. Since they cannot allow themselves that luxury any longer, many use force to do so... Ours is now a country of empty schools. In Venezuela, an armed adolescent underworld rules over the outer suburbs of a capital city of 4 million people. The inhabitants of the wealthy areas have barricaded themselves in. Or they block off streets to divert the traffic towards sentry boxes where guards pick out the supposed wrongdoers. These are hardened criminals — fearsome, cruel youngsters who destroy merely for the sake of doing so... Our moral crisis is the result of widespread corruption. The reason for this corruption is the example set by political leaders, bankers, company bosses... They have been mixed up in so many corruption scandals that they have lost all credibility... The people on the fringes of society are trying to get their hands on everything those others have obtained illegally: houses, women, liquor, food, yachts, planes, trips. And what they got through crooked means the fringe dwellers get through violence.

Juan Jesús Aznárez, El País, August 1995, Madrid

'*the moral foundation disintegrating before our eyes is not this solid mass of old-fashioned morality in which all spheres are intermingled, but the historical outcome — the sediment of ethos — of all our ethical efforts... [Thus] the real debate is not between religion and ethics, but between a religion that makes ethics possible, even necessary, and a religion that makes ethics impossible, superfluous and therefore diabolical, although it exists even so.*'[10]

There is a genuine desire for consensus today in international population negotiations. The problem, however, is the substance of a consensus because 'although there is agreement about the fundamental principles of human dignity and the respect owed to the human person, there is no agreement about the ontological foundation of those values and therefore no agreement about the limits to the applicability of the principles'.[11] Thus, given the systematic doubt bedevilling us and the lack of an incontrovertible universal foundation, should we perhaps accept that the ethical dimension derives 'less from strength and assertion than from uncertainty and disarray? Understood in this way, ethics neither legislates nor theorizes; it is the ethics of uncertainty in that the call for "ethicalness" may arise also out of hesitation and uncertainty.'[12]

Ethical Requirements

Ethical issues open up a vast field of requirements, and we make no claim here to identify all aspects of them. Several, however, are immediately identifiable from what was said earlier about the international negotiations.

┌─ *In the news* ──┐

Reality

Here's some good news! The number of robberies and burglaries in 1994 is falling. That gave me a start when I read it in Le Monde... *The Police Commissioner's crime statistics had been in my head for several months before I realized that low figures meant there had been too many burglaries. They announce the first burglary and perhaps the second one, and then they give up... I am amazed by what is happening: we are losing touch with reality. Nowadays, we see the world only through statistics, graphs and information, and we think that is reality, ... there is nowhere any more where people tell the truth, ... we are going to go completely mad, which is a lot worse than being burgled.*

Catherine Flament, Le Monde, *March 1995, Paris*

└──┘

The primary requirement, upon which all others depend, is to use concrete language to describe individual experience, and to enable it to manifest itself by restoring the balance in the power of problem definition. It is becoming increasingly clear that if we approach population challenges from an ethical standpoint, we are obliged to ask ourselves whether what is said and who says it are legitimate. This is applicable to, for example, industrialized countries defining the rules of world trade, the Anglo-Saxon approach setting population policy priorities for the countries of the South, technocratic powers dictating social security mechanisms, and the doctor (not the patient) deciding whether the patient is to live or die. This approach imposes three conditions. First, we have to change the present pattern of competition into one of mutual assistance and assumption of responsibility. Second, we have to apprehend problems with verbal accuracy so as to come as close as possible to the reality of life as it is lived and perceived by the people concerned. Third, we must not deny conflicts but endeavour to overcome them by removing obstacles through the proper use of words. The language of myths is often infinitely more powerful than the language of diplomacy. An illustration of this comes from the cultural heritage of the Lissou mountain people. 'Long, long ago, in ancestral times, women wore their apron in front, whereas men wore theirs at the back. That is why women were intelligent and men stupid. One day, a wise man happened to pass by. He advised the men to wear their apron in front like the women. They heeded his advice, and from that day forth they were intelligent.'[13]

Notes and References

Introduction

1 René Passet, 'La crise économique dans le courant de l'évolution', in *Du cosmos à l'Homme*, L'Harmattan, 1991, p. 49.

2 Rubens Ricupero, Secretary-General of the United Nations Conference on Trade and Development (UNCTAD), *Le Monde*, 24–25 December 1995, p. 2.

3 André Rougemont, *Sozial- und Präventivmedizin*, Birkhäuser Verlag, Basel, Vol. 40, No. 1, 1995, p. 4.

Chapter 1

1 Jean-Claude Chasteland, 'La croissance de la population mondiale devant la communauté et l'opinion internationales', *Revue française des Affaires sociales*, Vol. 48, No. 4, October–December 1994.

2 Ibid., p. 2.

3 United Nations, *The future growth of world population*, 1959, XIII, 2.

4 Now called the United Nations Population Fund. Although the name has been simplified, the acronym remains unchanged.

5 UN General Assembly resolution 3019 of 18 December 1972, XXVII.

6 Joaquín Arango, 'Tempestad sobre el Cairo', *Claves de razón práctica*, No. 49, December 1994, p. 27.

7 Martha M. Campbell, 'Schools of thought: negotiation analysis applied to interest groups active in international population policy formulation', discussion paper, Population Association of America, April 1993.

8 Ibid.

9 C. Alison McIntosh and Jason L. Finkle, 'The Cairo Conference on Population and Development: a new paradigm?', *Population and Development Review*, 21, No. 2, June 1995,

p. 236.

10 Ibid., p. 239.

11 Christophe Ayad, 'Le *oui mais* du Vatican aux débats du Caire', *Libération*, 14 September 1994.

Chapter 2

1 François Jacob, *Le jeu des possibles*, Fayard, Paris, 1981, pp. 127–128.

2 In France in the eighteenth century, and in present-day Turkey and Japan. See *inter alia* Cem Behar, 'Une transition démographique presque achevée: le cas de la Turquie', in Jean-Claude Chasteland and Jean-Claude Chesnais (eds), *La population mondiale*, Cahiers de l'INED, forthcoming.

3 Huda Zurayk, Nabil Younis and Hind Khattab, 'Rethinking family planning in light of reproductive health research', *The Policy Series, Reproductive Health*, No. 1, Population Council, Regional Office for West Asia and North Africa, Cairo.

4 Dominique Tabutin and M. Willems, 'La surmortalité des filles jusqu'en 1940: un bel exemple des inégalités sexuelles dans l'histoire occidentale', *Chaire Quetelet 1994*, Louvain-la-Neuve, forthcoming.

5 Hervé Le Bras, 'La peur du nombre', interview given to Nicolas Journet, *Sciences humaines*, No. 50, May 1995.

6 A common practice in some African societies whereby children are lent or adopted by a family with which they do not necessarily have any direct biological links.

7 *The New Catechism.*

8 E. Bertholet, 'Adoptive rights and reproductive wrongs', in G. Sen and R. C. Snow, *Power and decision: the social control of reproduction*, Harvard Center for Population and Development Studies, 1994.

9 Allan G. Hill, 'Truth lies in the eye of the beholder: the nature of evidence in demography and anthropology', paper presented at the Conference on Anthropological Demography, Brown University, Rhode Island, November 1994, forthcoming.

10 J. Wood, 'Fertility in anthropological populations', *Annual Review of Anthropology*, 19, 1994, pp. 211–242.

11 Ibid.

12 See Alfred Perrenoud's contribution, pp. 38–41.

13 M. Minali-Comparetti, 'Birth control and ethical questions', report of the symposium on this subject, Inter-Congrès des sciences anthropologiques et ethnologiques, Florence, April 1995, forthcoming in the *Journal of Bioethics*.

14 See Joel Jakubec's contribution, pp. 123–125.

15 Guy Bugault, *L'Inde pense-t-elle?*, PUF, Paris, 1994.

16 Ibid., pp. 64–65.

17 Pierre de Locht, *Morale sexuelle et magistère*, Éditions du Cerf, Paris, 1992, pp. 246–247.

18 Paul Valadier, interviewed by Henri Tincq, *Le Monde*, 28–29 May 1995, p. 11.

19 Alaka Basu, 'Family size and child welfare in an urban slum: some disadvantages of being poor but "modern"', *Fertility, family size and structure consequences for families and children*,

Proceedings of a Population Council Seminar, Population, June 1992, Population Council, New York, 1993; 'The status of women and the quality of life among the poor', *Cambridge Journal of Economics*, 1992, 16, pp. 249–267; 'Women's economic roles and child survival: the case of India', *Health Transition Review*, Vol. 1, No. 1, 1991, pp. 83–108.

20 Frédéric de Coninck and Francis Godard, 'Itinéraires familiaux, itinéraires profession-nels: vers de nouvelles biographies féminines', *Sociologie du travail*, No. 1/92, pp. 65–79.

21 Jean-Claude Chesnais, *La démographie*, PUF, Paris, 1990.

22 Jean-Pierre Olivier de Sardan, 'Séniorité et citoyenneté en Afrique pré-coloniale', *Communications*, EHESS-CNRS, Marseilles, p. 120.

Chapter 3

1 At the Vienna Conference on Human Rights in 1992 the industrialized countries accepted this new right in exchange for continued acceptance of the universality of individual rights, which were challenged particularly by Asian countries. Experience shows that a concept based on political compromise is rarely a precise one.

2 Walter Mertens, 'The 1994 ICPD: context and characteristics', *IUSSP Policy and Research Papers*, No. 7, 1995, pp. 16–17.

3 Pierre Encrevé, 'L'homme politique et son discours sont-ils des produits?', interview, *Cahiers protestants*, No. 5, Geneva, October 1993, p. 5.

4 See Chapter 6.

5 Harriet Presser, *PAA Affairs*, Spring 1991.

6 This breakdown does not include the work of economists.

7 Paul Demeny, *Population and development*, ICPD series, IUSSP, Liège, 1994, pp.19–20.

8 Massimo Livi-Bacci, *Pauvreté et population*, ICPD series, IUSSP, Liège, 1994, p. 11.

9 Jacques Véron, *Arithmétique de l'homme: la démographie entre science et politique*, Éditions du Seuil, 1993, pp. 145–147. See also Robert Franck (under the direction of), *Faut-il chercher aux raisons une cause? L'explication causale dans les sciences humaines*, Institut interdisciplinaire d'études épistémologiques, Lyons, and Librairie philosophique, J. Vrin, Paris, 1994.

10 Livi-Bacci, op. cit., p. 17.

11 Bruno Lautier, 'Les malheureux sont les puissants de la terre: représentations et régula-tions étatiques de la pauvreté en Amérique latine', *GREITD-IEDES*, Paris, November 1993.

12 Demeny, op. cit., p. 21.

13 Guy Herzlich, 'Les inégalités de revenus s'accentuent dans les pays industrialisés', *Le Monde*, 29–30 October 1995, p. 5.

14 Hubert Greppin, 'Anomie écologique et société urbaine', *Médecine et Hygiène*, No. 42, 1984, p. 3644; and text from *Certificat international du Centre européen d'écologie humaine*, No. 17.

15 Samuel Preston, 'Are the economic consequences of population growth a sound basis for population policy?', in Jane Menken (ed.), *World population & U.S. policy: the choices ahead*, W. W. Norton, New York, 1986, p. 69.

16 G. McNicoll and M. Cain, 'Institutional effects on rural economic and demographic change', *Rural development and population: institutions and policies* (G. McNicoll and M. Cain, eds), *Population and Development Review*, supplement to Vol. 15, 1989, pp. 3–42.

17 FAO, *World agriculture: towards 2010* (N. Alexandratos, ed.), John Wiley & Sons, Chichester.

18 Approximately 90 million hectares should be added to the 760 million hectares currently under cultivation.

19 This index is currently about 0.8 for the developing countries as whole: 0.55 in Africa, but 1.12 in South Asia. It should rise to 0.85 in 2010.

20 In the developing countries it will have to rise from 62 kilograms per hectare to 110 kilograms per hectare.

21 A hypothesis about the income of the agricultural population (about 40 per cent of the world population) is basically a hypothesis about the level of agricultural output.

22 1 calorie = 1 kcal, i.e. 1000 calories.

23 The FAO put the number of undernourished people at 786 million for the period 1988-1990. The net result would therefore be an approximately 19 per cent reduction of that number within twenty years. See FAO, *Nutrition and development: a global assessment*, Rome, 1992.

24 Approximately 70 per cent of world consumption and 90 per cent in low-income countries.

25 Water availability is more than a physical fact: it is a function of the cost of supplying water where and when needed, in the requisite quantity and of the requisite quality. This cost increases rapidly in situations of relative scarcity, hence the importance of the population–water resources ratio.

26 E. Engelman and P. Leroy, *Sustaining water: population and the future of renewable water supplies*, Population Action International, Washington DC, 1993.

27 90 per cent of which was for the populations of those regions that have been dry since the beginning of the 1990s, particularly those of the sub-Saharan region.

28 A.-M. Bonfiglioli, *Pastoralists at the crossroads: survival and development issues in African pastoralism*, UNICEF/UNSO, Nopa, Nairobi, 1992; I. Livingstone, *Pastoralism: an overview of practices, process and policy*, FAO, Rome, 1995.

29 G. Hardin, 'The tragedy of the commons', *Science*, No. 162, 1968, pp. 1243–1245.

30 UNEP, *Situation en ce qui concerne la désertification et la mise en oeuvre du plan d'action des Nations Unies pour lutter contre la désertification*, Nairobi, 1992; C. Sommerville, 'Drought and aid in the Sahel: a decade of development cooperation', in *Westview Special Studies on Africa*, Westview Press, Boulder, Colorado, 1986.

31 ICIHI (Independent Commission on International Humanitarian Issues), *The encroaching desert: the consequences of human failure*, Zed Books, London, 1986; M. K. Tolba, 'Harvest of dust', *Desertification Control Bulletin*, No. 10, 1984.

32 J. Swift, *Major issues in pastoral development with special emphasis on selected African countries*, FAO, Rome, 1988; S. Sandford, *Management of pastoral development in the Third World*, ODI/John Wiley, London, 1983.

33 J.-P. Jacob, 'Entre décentralisation et désengagement: principes et problèmes de l'auto-organisation paysanne en Africa', in *Jeux et enjeux de l'auto-promotion*, PUF-IUED, Paris and Geneva, 1991, pp. 41–48.

Chapter 4

1 Joseph-Alfred Grinblat, 'Le vieillissement des populations mondiales: tendances démographiques récentes et futures', in M. Loriaux, D. Remy and E. Vilquin (under the direction of), *Populations âgées et révolution grise: les hommes et les sociétés face à leurs vieillissements*, Chaire Quetelet 1986, Éditions Ciaco, Brussels, pp. 53–76.

2 I. Beyens-Wu, 'Ageing in a changing population: China in the twenty-first century', *Chaire Quetelet 1986*, pp. 177–189.

3 Patrice Bourdelais, 'Le vieillissement de la population: question d'actualité ou notion obsolète?', *Le débat: histoire, politique, société*, No. 82, November–December 1994.

4 Jean-Pierre Michel and Jean-Marie Robine, in Bourdelais, op. cit.

5 Professor of Demography, University of Montreal.

6 Hermann-Michel Hagmann, 'Plaidoyer pour une politique nouvelle des âges', in *Standpunkte zwischen Theorie und Praxis*, Haupt, Bern, 1995. See also Jean Kellerhals, Josette Coenen-Huther, Malik von Allmen and Hermann-Michel Hagmann, 'Proximité affective et entraide entre générations: la génération-pivot et ses pères et mères', *Gérontologie et société. Cahiers de la Fondation nationale de gérontologie*, Paris, No. 68, 1994.

7 Dominique Tabutin, 'L'âge vermeil du tiers Monde: perspectives des populations âgées dans les pays jeunes', *Chaire Quetelet 1986*.

8 Gildas Simon, 'Des mondes en mouvement', *Libération*, special supplement, 1995.

9 Ibid.

10 Alfred Perrenoud, 'La migration en Europe entre le XIIIe et le XVIIIe siècles', Institut international d'histoire économique F. Datini-Prato, May 1993, p. 884.

11 *Preliminary Documents*, p. 216.

12 Nothing has been invented!

13 32nd Inter-Parliamentary Conference, *Proceedings*, pp. 521–522. Statistics of the International Labour Organization indicate that in 1936 the number of jobless in Western Europe totalled 25 million; this figure did not include farmers, who were largely underemployed owing to changes in the rural economy.

14 35 million unemployed in the OECD countries and 11 per cent of Western Europe's working population.

15 Also known as unplanned urbanization.

16 Owing to the increase in fossil energy used for transport purposes.

17 Jacques Vallin, *La population mondiale*, La Découverte, 1995.

18 Ibid., p. 94.

19 Jacques Vallin, 'Réflexions sur l'avenir de la population mondiale', *Dossiers du CEPED*, No. 26, May 1994, Paris.

20 Jean-Marc Ela, *Chaire Quetelet 1990*, p. 65. In actual fact, Africa's population in 2050 will be approximately 2.1 billion, not 1 billion.

Chapter 5

1 It is available from the United Nations Population Division in New York.

2 OECD, Development Assistance Committee, Meeting on Population and Development, 29–30 November 1994, AC report, OECD/GD (95) 37, Paris, 1995.

3 Jacques Schwartz, 'Population et développement, un vieux couple', interview by Pascal Biston, *Courier de la Planète*, No. 25, November–December 1994, p. 5.

4 Philippe Lemaître, 'Le respect des droits de l'homme, élément essentiel des relations de l'Europe avec ses anciennes colonies', *Le Monde*, 5–6 November 1995, p. 3.

5 This is far from being the case at the present time, as the industrialized countries' commercial interests still generally take precedence over the ethics of international relations.

6 Sophia Mappa, 'Le développement par la démocratie?', *Le Débat*, No. 83, January–February 1995, pp. 59–83.

7 Ibid.

8 Daniel Vernet, 'Nationaux de tous les pays, séparez-vous!', *Le Monde*, 7 June 1995.

9 Jean-Pierre Jacob, François Margot, Paul Sauvain and Peter Uvin (in collaboration with Christophe Dunand and Philippe Chauvin), *Guide d'approche des institutions locales: méthodologie d'étude des acteurs locaux dans le monde rural*, Institut universitaire d'études du développement, Itinéraires, Notes et Travaux, No. 40, Geneva, March 1994.

10 Council of Europe, Recommendation 381 of 16 January 1964.

11 Council of Europe, Notice No. 47 of 28 April 1967.

12 One of Georges Corm's books is entitled *The new world economic disorder (Le nouveau désordre économique mondial)*, La Découverte, Paris, 1993.

13 *The reality of aid*, ICVA–Eurostep, June 1993.

14 Christian Giordano, 'Les migrants et les non-migrants du Mezzogiorno', in *Vers un ailleurs prometteur: l'émigration, une réponse universelle à une situation de crise*, PUF/Cahiers de l'IUED, 1993, p. 353.

15 Jean Chesneaux, 'Rééquilibrage Nord-Sud' *Transversales*, No. 32, p. 34.

Chapter 6

1 DAC Report, OECD/GD (95) 37, Paris 1995.

2 According to a study by Tint International, Brussels, for UNFPA. See also Roberta Rossi and Angela Silvestrini, 'La conférence du Caire vue par la presse néderlandaise, italienne et tchèque: une synthèse', communication to the European Demography Congress, Milan, 4–8 September 1995.

3 Alain Desrosières, 'Démographie, science et société: le cas français', communication presented to the International Symposium '1945-1995: Half a Century of Population Research', INED, Paris, October 1995.

4 Ibid., p. 4.

5 Ibid., p. 7.

6 Samuel Preston, 'Where is US demography headed?', communication presented to the International Symposium, '1945-1995: Half a Century of Population Research', INED, Paris, October 1995, pp. 7–8.

7 Research concentrated initially on Asia and Latin America, regions then at the heart of American political interests.

8 Simon Szreter, 'The idea of demographic transition and the study of fertility change: a critical intellectual history', *Population and Development Review*, No. 4-19, 1993, p. 682.

9 Physical capital includes infrastructures and producer goods.

10 Jean-Claude Chasteland, 'La croissance de la population mondiale devant la communauté et l'opinion internationales', *Revue française des affaires sociales*, Vol. 48, No. 4, October–December 1994.

11 Dennis A. Ahlburg, *Independent inquiry report into population and development* (commissioned by the Australian Government), April 1994.

12 'Population and economic development', *Report by the group of expert economists*, organized by UNFPA, September 1992, New York, p. 57.

13 Ivo Rens, 'En quoi les idées politiques de Théodore de Bèze et des monarchomaques protestants innovèrent-elles?', in *Jacques Godefroy (1587–1652) et l'Humanisme juridique à Genève*, Helbing & Lichtenhahn, and Law Faculties of Geneva, Basel and Frankfurt, 1991, p. 179.

14 Paul-F. Geisendorf, *Théodore de Bèze*, Labor et Fides, Geneva, 1949, p. 315.

15 Alain Perrot, 'L'attitude de Jean Calvin face à la science', in *Charles Bonnet savant et philosophe (1720–1793). Mémoires de la Société de physique et d'histoire naturelle de Genève*, Vol. 47, 1994, p. 268.

16 Pierre Chaunu (ed.), *L'aventure de la Réforme*, Desclée de Brouwer, Paris, 1986, p. 265.

17 Sermon CXXXVII on Deuteronomy.

18 UNFPA, *Population and development strategies*, Technical Report, New York, 1993.

19 Michel Loriaux, Chaire Quetelet, p. 14.

20 Dominique Tabutin and Evelyne Thiltges, 'Relations entre croissance démographique et environnement: du doctrinal à l'empirique', *Revue Tiers Monde*, Vol. XXXIII, No. 130, April–June 1992.

21 Paul Demeny, *Population and development*, IUSSP, CIPD series, Liège 1994, p. 15.

22 Jean-Claude Chasteland, 'L'intégration des variables démographiques dans la planification du développement aux Nations unies: contenu politique et technique du concept', in H. Gérard (ed.), *Intégrer population et développement, Chaire Quetelet 1990*, Academia-L'Harmattan, Louvain-la-Neuve, 1993.

23 Demeny, op. cit.

24 René Passet, 'La mutation économique: du territoire à l'éthique', *Transversales*, No. 26, March–April 1994, p. 16.

25 Immanuel Wallerstein, *Unthinking social sciences: the limits of nineteenth century paradigms*, Polity Press, Cambridge, UK, 1991.

26 Ibid., p. 105.

27 Ibid., p. 122

28 *Focus on humankind: new agenda for sustainable development*, report of a colloquium held in Stockholm in November 1994, Cabinet Office and Ministries, Stockholm, 1994, p. 26.

Chapter 7

1 Alex Mauron, 'La génétique humaine et le souci des générations futures', *Folia Bioethica*, No. 14, Société suisse d'éthique biomédicale, Geneva, 1993, p. 6.

2 Armand Delsemme, *Les origines cosmiques de la vie: du Big Bang à l'Homme*, Nouvelle bibliothèque scientifique, Flammarion, Paris, 1994, p. 322.

3 Isabelle Stengers, 'La complexité: une mode et/ou un besoin'; in *Du cosmos à l'Homme*, L'Harmattan, 1991, pp. 79–117.

4 Robert Castel, *Les métamorphoses de la question sociale*, Fayard, Paris, 1995, p. 461.

5 Pierre Gilliand and Pascal Mahon, 'La sécurité sociale dans une société en mutation', in *Rapport au Conseil de l'Europe*, Lausanne, August 1988, p. 17.

6 Dominique Tabutin, 'Transitions démographiques et société', *Chaire Quetelet 1992*, Louvain-la-Neuve, forthcoming.

7 René Passet, 'La crise économique dans le courant de l'évolution', in *Du cosmos à l'Homme*, pp. 52–53.

8 René Passet, 'Les voies d'une économie plurielle', *Transversales*, special issue, No. 32, March–April 1995, p. 4.

9 K. Hakem, quoted by René Passet in *Une économie de rêve*, Calmann-Lévy, Paris, 1995.

10 I. Serageldin, 'Making development sustainable', *Finance and Development*, Vol. 30, No. 4, 1993, pp. 6–10; Robert Goodland, *Environmental sustainability and the power sector*, The World Bank, Washington DC, 1994; Hydro-Quebec Conference on Sustainable Development, Montreal, 6 September 1994.

11 See Arrow's famous impossibility theorem, which demonstrates the impossibility of constructing a social utility or well-being function: Kenneth J. Arrow, 'Alternative approaches to the theory of choice in risk-taking situations', *Econometrica*, No. 19, 1951, pp. 404–437.

12 Known as the Kaldor-Hicks principle.

13 It should be noted in this connection that the United States, which is quick to preach world population stabilization, has not deemed it necessary to stabilize its own population, which rose from 152 million in 1950 to 261 million in 1994 and will probably reach 349 million in 2050. This would make the United States the most populous industrial nation over the whole period. See J. Vallin, *La population mondiale*, La Découverte, Paris, p. 93.

14 K. J. Arrow, J. Parikh and G. J. Pillet, *Decision-making framework for addressing climate change, Second IPCC Assessment Report*, Cambridge University Press, 1996.

15 N. Choucri (ed.), *Global accord*, MIT Press, Cambridge, Mass., 1993. See also N. Choucri, 'Introduction', *Business & the Contemporary World*, Vol. 2, 1994, pp. 6–7.

16 Jerome Rothenberg, 'Economic perspective on time comparisons: evaluation of time discounting', in *Global accord*, pp. 307–332.

17 Sylvie Faucheux and Géraldine Frogger, 'Decision-making under environmental uncertainty', in *Steps towards a decision-making framework to address climate change* (under the direction of G. Pillet and F. Gassmann), Paul Scherrer Institut (PSI-Bericht, No. 94–10), Würenlingen, Switzerland, 1994, pp. 51–65.

18 G. Pillet, op. cit., 'Betting on climate states', pp. 115–137, and Andrea Beltratti, op. cit., 'Environmental problems and attitudes towards risk and uncertainty', pp. 67-74.

19 Howard Thomas Odum, *Systems ecology*, Wiley, New York, 1983. See also G. Pillet and H. T. Odum, *E3: énergie, écologie, économie*, Georg, Geneva, 1987.

20 Graciela Chichilnisky, 'Global environmental risks and financial instruments', in *Steps towards a decision-making framework to address climate change*, pp. 99–114.

21 See the work of Arrow and Debreu in the 1950s. Although the idea of 'Arrow's securities' dates back to the 1950s, the application of the theory underlying it to international markets dates from the beginning of the 1990s, along with risks related to climate change. Its application to demographic change is proposed here, probably for the first time.

22 E. Manzini, 'Values, quality and sustainable development: the role of the cultural factor in the environmental reorientation of the system of production and consumption', in Tim Jackson (ed.), *Clean production strategies: developing preventive environmental management in the industrial economy*, Stockholm Environment Institute and Lewis Publishers, 1993, p. 372.

23 Paul Ricoeur, 'Éthique et responsabilité', in Jean-Christophe Aeschlimann (ed.), *Éditions de la Baconnière*, Collection 'Langages', Neuchâtel, Switzerland, 1994, p. 12.

Conclusion

1 René Passet, 'La mutation économique: du territoire à l'éthique', *Transversales*, No. 26, March–April 1994, p. 16.

2 Monique Castillo, 'De la bioéthique à l'éthique', *Esprit*, July 1995, p. 86.

3 Dominique Folscheid, 'Pour une philosophie de l'écologie', *Éthique, la vie en question*, No. 13, 1994/3, p. 14.

4 Odile Bourguignon, 'Problèmes éthiques posés par la psychanalyse et l'étude du psychisme humain', *Éthique, la vie en question*, No. 15, 1995/1, p. 95.

5 Dieter Birnbacher, *La responsabilité envers les générations futures*, PUF, Paris, 1994, pp. 16, 88–89 and 124–126.

6 Hans Jonas, *Le principe de responsabilité: une éthique pour la civilisation technologique*, Éditions du Cerf, Paris, 1993, p. 62.

7 Joel Jakubec, 'Éthique et écologie', in *Stratégies énergétiques, biosphère et sociétés*, Éditions Médecine et Hygiène, Geneva, 1991, pp. 63–69.

8 Castillo, op. cit., p. 105.

9 Ibid., p. 109.

10 Dominique Folscheid, 'Les démons de l'éthique', *Éthique, la vie en question*, No. 15, 1995/1, pp. 10–11.

11 Castillo, op. cit., p. 93.

12 Ibid., p. 106.

13 Tales of the Lissou (Tibeto-Burman) mountain people, gathered orally by William Dessaint and Avòunado Ngwama, in *Au sud des nuages: l'aube des peuples*, Gallimard, 1994, p. 645.

Index

Page numbers in **bold** refer to figures and tables

child marriage 28
child mortality
  girls 26
  recommendations in PAPD 20
childbirth *see* pregnancy and childbirth
children
  child's place in family 35
  diseases 16
  needs, recommendations in PAPD 33–4
  recommendations in PAPD 20–1
  restriction of numbers per couple 38
  and women's work 43–5
China
  cultural misunderstandings 109
  population ageing 75, 76
  population growth 91
cities *see* urbanization
closed-loop production cycle **147**
collective negotiation **141**
collective responsibility 150, 152–3
community groups, recommendations in PAPD 21
competition, pattern of, problem of 155
component manufacturing 148, 149
Conference on Population and Development *see*
  Cairo conference (1994)
'conference system' of negotiation xiv–xv
consumerism
  and fertility rates 40
  and population growth 61–2
contraception 16
  in Africa 46
  differences between countries 36
  medicalized 35–7
  relationship to birth control 35
  and sexual behaviour 24–5
contraceptives
  for sexually transmitted diseases, reservations **8**
  supply, reservations **8**
  see also family planning
costs of child-rearing 19
Council of Europe 105–6
couples
  concept of couple, discussion at regional
    conferences 13
  recommendations in PAPD **12**
  reservations on terminology used in PAPD **8**
cultural interpretations
  of empowerment **10**
  of gender **29**
  misunderstandings 109, 122–3
  see also national differences
cultural values, rights and 4

danger areas, environmental risks worldwide **136**
decision-making 135–8
'dematerialization' of products 146, 148

democracy
  importance in PAPD 98, 99–101
  participatory, PAPD 96
demographic change, framework for 140–1
demographic development, view of Cairo conference 129
demographic input to Cairo conference 12–13
demographic perspective 133
demographic structure, recommendations in
  PAPD **12**
demographic transition 116–17, 126
dependency, threshold of 76
desertification, problems of 66–9
development
  essential measures 50–1
  as focus of Cairo conference 11, 113, **113**, 114
  meaning 128
  and politics 56
  and population 49–69, 126–7
  and population dynamics, recommendations in
    PAPD 14
  right to 49–50, 54–7
  theory of 117–19
disabilities, people with *see* people with disabilities
discounting, and demographic change 142
discrimination against women 20, 29
  from birth 26
diseases
  global mortality 73
  incidence 73
dualistic approach to solutions 125

Earth Summit xiv, 5
  attitudes to population and development 68
East Asia, elderly population **77**
Eastern Europe, relocation of aid to 107
ecological aspects of population change 52, 144
  objectives, related to social and economic
    objectives **139**
  see also environment
economic development
  and democracy 99
  recommendations in PAPD **12**
economic disintegration, example 135
economic growth
  and population 133–5
  role of 56, 127–8
  stimulation to combat poverty 50, 52–4
  and sustainable development 9
economic objectives
  related to social and ecological objectives **139**
  sustainable 145
economic requirements, need for redefinition 137
economics
  closed-loop production cycle **147**
  corruption, and crime 154

Other relevant publications from Earthscan

The Politics of Population
The International Conference on Population and Development, Cairo 1994
Stanley Johnson

The Cairo conference represented a definitive change in the world's approach to the population crisis. Not only was there unprecedented consensus among the 179 countries taking part, but it also created a wide-ranging Programme of Action which for the first time offers a real chance of progress by putting population policies at the heart of social development. The Programme of Action is probably one of the most important social documents of our time, Stanley Johnson captures the drama and detail of its creation.

£14.95 *paperback* ISBN 1 85383 297 9

The Future Population of the World
What Can We Assume Today? Second Edition
Edited by Wolfgang Lutz

The highly acclaimed *The Future Population of the World* contains the most authoritative assessment available of the extent to which population is likely to grow over the next 50 to 100 years. The book provides a thorough analysis of all the components of population change and translates these factors into a series of projections for the population of the world's regions. This revised and updated version incorporates completely new scenario projections based on updated starting values and revised assumptions, plus several methodological improvements. It also contains the best currently available information on global trends in AIDS mortality and the first ever fully probabilistic world population projections.

£24.95 *paperback* ISBN 1 85383 349 5   £50.00 *hardback* ISBN 1 85383 344 4

Population and Strategies for National Sustainable Development
A Guide to Assist National Policy Makers in Linking Population and Environment in Strategies for Sustainable Development
Gayl D Ness with Meghan V Golay, for IUCN and UNFPA

This book, prepared by the World Conservation Union and the United Nations Fund for Population Activities, explains the links between population dynamics and sustainable development in ways which will enable planners and policy makers to build them into strategies for national sustainable development.

£13.95 *paperback* ISBN 1 85383 375 4

The Earthscan Reader in Population and Development
Edited by Paul Demeny and Geoffrey McNicoll

This comprehensive selection of essays cuts through the technical literature to provide an accessible guide to the complex issues surrounding population and development. It will be invaluable to students requiring a complete text for courses in population studies as well as development, sociology, geography and environmental courses.

Leading writers including Kingsley Davis, Herman Daly, Gary Becker, Ester Boesrup and Amartya Sen, and many others, discuss the major themes of population and development.

£19.95 *paperback* ISBN 1 85383 275 8   £45.00 *hardback* ISBN 1 85383 474 2

People Who Count
Population and Politics, Women and Children
Dorothy Stein

Dorothy Stein confronts the contentious political issues on all sides of the population debate, including immigration, demographic competition, gender ratios, reproductive research and children's rights. She argues that lower fertility rates are preferred by women themselves and are beneficial in their own right to both women and children. Drawing on research in anthropology, child psychology and population studies she presents a challenging case for policies which recognize hopeful trends in relieving the environmental and social pressures of an increasing global population.

£13.95 *paperback* ISBN 1 85383 233 2

Who Will Feed China?
Wake-up Call for a Small Planet
Lester R Brown

The latest book in the Worldwatch Environment Alert Series addresses the implications of China's increasing food consumption. As the record pace of industrialization raises Chinese living standards, and consumes large areas of agricultural land, China is facing a grain deficit so large it could overwhelm the export capacity of North America and other exporting nations. The resulting competition will drive up prices with potentially disastrous consequences for the world's poor.

£9.95 *paperback* ISBN 1 85383 316 9

Changing the Boundaries
Women-Centered Perspectives on Population and the Environment
Janice Jiggins

Explores gender relations with respect to education, reproductive health services, and agricultural resources - three factors that are recognized as being central to the struggle for gender equity, population control, and environmental sustainability. Data, arguments, concepts, and analysis from a wide range of sources are woven together to link the experience of women's daily lives with population policies and global environmental politics.

£16.95 *paperback* ISBN 1 55963 260 7

Beyond the Numbers
A Reader on Population, Consumption and the Environment
Edited by Laurie Ann Mazur

Presents a thought-provoking series of essays by leading authorities on issues of population and consumption. Chapters consider each of the broad topics addressed at the 1994 International Conference on Population and Development.

£18.95 *paperback* ISBN 1 55963 299 2

All our People
Population Policy with a Human Face
Klaus Leisinger with Karin Schmitt, for ICPD/UNICEF

All our People provides an in-depth, balanced treatment of such factors as human consumption patterns, the ethical issues surrounding population policy, and the role of women in development issues. The authors consider the wide range of conditions necessary to mitigate problems associated with population growth and the environment.

£19.95 *paperback* ISBN 1 55963 293 3

Earthscan Publications Ltd
http://www.earthscan.co.uk